ST. FRANCIS XAVIER

ST. FRANCIS
XAVIER

Jean-Marc
Montguerre

TRANSLATED BY RUTH MURDOCH

Doubleday & Company, Inc., Garden City, New York

1963

Nihil obstat: Gall Higgins, O. F. M. Cap.
               Censor Librorum

Imprimatur:✠ Francis Cardinal Spellman
               Archbishop of New York
               June 27, 1963

The *nihil obstat* and *imprimatur* are official declarations that a book or pamphlet is free of doctrinal or moral error. No implication is contained therein that those who have granted the *nihil obstat* and *imprimatur* agree with the contents, opinions or statements expressed.

This is a translation of *François Xavier au Quartier Latin* and *François Xavier dans les Chemins d'Orient* (Paris: Editions France-Empire, 68 Rue Jean-Jacques Rousseau, Paris, 1960)

Library of Congress Catalog Card Number 63–18222
Copyright © 1963 by Doubleday & Company, Inc.
All Rights Reserved
Printed in the United States of America
First Edition

ST. FRANCIS XAVIER

I

In the little fortress of Xavier, whipped by the winds of the parched Basque valleys, Maria de Azpicuelta gave birth, on April 7, 1506, to her sixth child and third son, Francis. We say that to see is the gift of womankind. God gives the Light. The Most High adapts to the most frail, and for Francis, born on Tuesday of Passion Week, the double gift was unique. Forty-six years later, near the Bay of Canton, his closing eyes would have seen the full glory of revealed Truth, with all earthly glories of land and sea, of scorched continents and luminous depths. All his ways—those of his soul and those of his marching feet—would know the full refraction of that which enlightens the destiny of man.

"Your useless Francis," he signs himself dispiritedly in one letter to Loyola. Hardly the appropriate term. His parents, wondering what the future held for their child, were to find him difficult, restless, proudly unyielding—and immediately attractive to others. He would be handsome and well built, with the lean vigor of a thoroughbred. In the absence of any portrait, numerous word-pictures acquaint us with the tall frame; the ready, sometimes aggressive, smile; the assurance, the kindliness of Francis Xavier. These characteristics were to remain unchanged as he went from one mode of existence to another: from childhood in the little family castle of Navarre, to student life, at the age of nineteen, in the University of Paris; and from Europe, at thirty-four, to his well-known apostolate in the countries of Asia. The boy racing over the sharp-stoned valleys of the Pyrenees, the student debating timely topics in the cramped houses of the Latin Quarter, and the great administrator of the missions share the same unchanged qualities and the same good nature.

Xavier—only the charming, the impulsive, the irresistible Francis was to have this austere title, determined for him by the will of a king. A village of lower Navarre had given its name to his father, Juan de Jassu, who, after completing his studies in law at Bologna, had been named to the council of John III of Navarre in the little capital of Pamplona. Shortly thereafter came Juan's marriage to Maria Azpicuelta. Since Maria, claiming descent from a ducal ancestor of the kings of Aragon, was the last of her family, John III resolved to transfer to Juan de Jassu the name and escutcheon of Azpicuelta. It was further agreed that their youngest son and his descendants should assume the title and arms of Xavier, recalling that the property and fortified castle had been a gift in the thirteenth century from Thibaut de Champagne. The King's final generosity to Don Juan, who like all country squires was something of a gentleman farmer, was to grant him civil jurisdiction over the adjacent lands and manor of Ydocin.

The castle of Xavier jutted out over the *rio* Aragon, an austere sentinel above an austere pass. It was a small, military construction, lifting a high yoke of gray walls from a firm basis of solid rock and serving as a protection to several farm buildings constructed against it. The little oratory of the fort, though nobly dedicated to Saint Michael, did not satisfy Juan, who endowed the Church of Santa Maria de Xavier with new dimensions and outlined for it regulations of an abbatial order. Minutely drawn up in fourteen parts, the rule required that Mass be sung every morning and the *Salve Regina* every night, with a Solemn High Mass on Sundays and holy days. The three poor chaplains of Xavier must strive to imitate the asceticism of the early saints, their only relaxation to be fishing in the rio or working in the garden. In all probability, these bucolic characters were the first masters of Francis and his brothers.

The spirit of Xavier's inhabitants corresponded to the appearance of the fort on its great rock between Heaven and earth. Life was comprised of duties to God and the work of the land. In some blocked-up passageway deep within the walls, they had found a Christ of pressed leather. The figure, concealed long before, possibly at a moment of threatened invasion by the Moors, lay detached from the cross and, with the arms in chains, was terrifying in its realism. The young child, Francis, was present at that somber operation that restored Christ to the cross, after which it was once again made an object of veneration.

Juan, however, did not forget his doctorate in law, and his time at Xavier was spent in litigations. Against feudal custom, he sent his great flock of merino sheep into the neighboring pastures of Sanguesa, and outraged townsmen brought the matter to justice. He moreover forbade any trespassing on his own land and kept one sheep out of any five so discovered. This gave rise to other discussions, and while Juan was confidently pleading his cause in Sanguesa, the confiscated beasts would be returned by a compassionate Maria as Francis and his brothers ran shouting through the white valley to recall the paternal flock.

Time passed. For the little kingdom of Navarre, three centuries of independence were to come to an end. From the heights of the dividing Pyrenees, each part seemed to incline naturally downwards towards the land of its own valleys.

Of the six children, Francis was by far the youngest. Maria, his oldest sister, had made her vows at the Abbey of Santa-Engracia in Pamplona. Madalena, the second, after a time spent as lady-in-waiting to Isabella of Castile, had joined the Poor Clares in Gandia. Ana, choosing a different submission, had married. The boys Miguel and Juan, contentious and daring, were learning to handle weapons, to hunt and fish with the chaplains. The child Francis, nine years younger than Juan, was less rugged and more emotional, closer in this way to his father. If he accompanied the chaplains, it was rather to their cells, for while neither a scholar nor an intellectual, he was thoughtfully reflective. With them, and perhaps with some Sanguesa tutor, he learned the rudiments of Latin, French, Italian, and Spanish, although his native tongue, which would come to his lips in delirium at Canton, was Basque.

In 1511, when Francis was only six, Navarre was forcibly incorporated into the Kingdom of Aragon by King Ferdinand. Pamplona was seized, and the King of Navarre, taking with him Juan de Jassu, escaped to Lumbier, across from Xavier, and from there into France. Juan, however, was not long in returning to his lands, his family, and his conquered state—only to see part of his property pre-empted and sold by Ferdinand. Although a few rights remained to him—for example, that of extracting one log from each load of timber floated down the Aragon—Juan was ruined, and in 1515 he died of grief. The exiled King of Navarre sent his widow seven hundred and ninety-one pounds, which, it must be said, were rightfully hers. Her note of acknowledgment is signed "the sorrowing Marya."

With the death of Ferdinand in the following year, Navarre rose in revolt. It was a naïve hope. The fearsome Cardinal Ximenes, as regent, had ordered all fortresses demolished. Xavier was gutted, but out of pity for Maria and her children, the Duke of Najera, viceroy of Navarre, spared the *casa*, or living quarters. Francis, who was ten at the time, saw the watchtowers crumble to the ground, leaving his child's horizon empty of its landmark. The emotions of such a boy, watching his family home destroyed by a squadron of soldiers, can well be imagined. There were many other grievances too. Peasants entered through forbidden approaches to cut down trees and remove fences so that the flocks of their former master would be lost. Gone then, indeed, was the time when Juan de Jassu, in the courtroom at Sanguesa, could cry out that the House of Xavier was one of the oldest and most privileged in Navarre.

Finally, the people of the *sierras* were tried beyond endurance. In 1516, when Charles V became Emperor of Spain, Navarre's place in the ensemble of European countries was even further reduced. The little kingdom of the Pyrenees made one last concerted effort. André de Foix, cousin of the exiled queen, Catherine of Navarre, came to their support at the head of a French army. Occupation troops had been withdrawn from Navarre because of difficulties in Castile, and Francis I, the young King of France, was delighted to play this trick on the Emperor, who was at that time in Germany.

Miguel and Juan de Jassu at once rallied the liberators, who were streaming down through Roncevaux after taking Saint Jean Pied-de-Port. Sanguesa was delivered on May 17, 1521, and the Duke of Najera fled to Pamplona, only to be overtaken on May 21. The attack was so violent that the garrison of the city was asked to surrender, but young Inigo de Loyola, a daredevil Basque nobleman fighting on the Castilian side, put the besieged to shame and became the spirit of the defense. When Inigo fell with a bullet through his right leg, however, the resistance was over. Pamplona surrendered.

Back at Xavier, Francis must have rejoiced over his brothers' success without realizing that it constituted a misfortune for one who twelve years later would be his friend and inspire his vocation. Inigo had been gravely wounded. On the advice of the best surgeons, the broken bones were reset several times. Historians have been led to speculate on what the result might have been for Francis if, indeed, Inigo had died at the time . . .

The French army had barely paraded through Pamplona, savoring the springtime—and the wines—of Navarre, when it met defeat at Noain. The Castilians reclaimed the capital. In the general stampede, Miguel de Jassu fled to hiding but was found and thrown into a dungeon. He escaped, doubtless helped by an accomplice in this country where his name still counted, and joined his brother Juan and the remaining Navarrese survivors in the old fortress of Fuenterrabía, which, dominating the sea opposite Hendaye, became the last resort for Navarre. The insurgents were courageous. Hearts continued to hold out where the dying could no longer speak or see. In the sumptuous golden city, whose name means "ford in the sands," their embattled resistance lasted for two years. On December 15, 1523, a weary Charles V gave general pardon to all but a few rebels—including Miguel and Juan de Jassu— whose blows had been notoriously telling. Firmly united, the Navarrese gave no answer. The Emperor, his patience at an end, withdrew the conditions in February of 1524, and the city was returned to him. The insurgents had been brave indeed, but the result was a definite mutilation for France.

Miguel and Juan went back to Xavier, where life returned to the *casa*. Only Juan, however, who settled comfortably into an easy life with an attractive wife, was to know the true "warrior's rest." Miguel died shortly after his own wedding.

Francis was eighteen. Listening to his brothers' tales, he

was shaken to realize that his own life up to then had been without any particular effort or challenge. Perhaps it was one of these late nights which stimulated the keen sense of ambition that was soon to possess him. A military career offered no temptation. He was sturdy and inured to hardship, but the army of Navarre was scattered, and it would hardly have occurred to Francis to put himself in the service of the Emperor. With his modest inheritance, he had no means of building up the farm lands of Azpicuelta, from which the family had been partially dispossessed. There remained the Church, and in it Francis saw his future. No humility inspired him; a young knight of illustrious birth might well carry the crosier, and most enviable titles came from the Catholic universities. In the hierarchy of the Church, he would find a sure satisfaction of his hopes. The thought of study at Alcala or Salamanca did not occur to him. The degree must be of unquestionable excellence. Bologna, where his father had studied, would not do. Nor would the most famous centers— Oxford, Pisa, Florence, Prague, Vienna, Toulouse, Caen. All were eclipsed by one alone—Paris, second only to the Holy See as the spiritual authority of Christendom.

Francis chose. The decision was important, even imprudent. Paris was very remote; distinction there was more dearly won than anywhere else. He would be without support, while closer to home, he might have benefited from the reputation of his cousin, Martin de Azpicuelta, a man of great learning and influence, who was advisor to the Emperor and professor of canon law. But with the loving encouragement of his sister in Gandia, Francis held to his choice and prepared for departure. As evidence of his vocation, and to insure an introduction—possibly also as a way of avoiding military service— he had himself named a cleric of the diocese of Pamplona. He put his affairs in order, appearing with his mother in the final arrangements for the rental of a mill—a fact which would seem to indicate that she, while waiting, had made him steward of the estate . . .

On a September morning in 1525, supplied with money for transportation and lodging in Paris, he rode off. He never again saw his mother, who died four years later, or any member of his family. When a child left home in those tragic days, it was usually understood that there would be no return.

II

Paris in 1525 was a bishopric of some four hundred thousand
souls, most of the agglomeration being spread out, as it is
today, along the right bank. The good city of Francis I, close
to becoming the heart of the kingdom now that the King was
to live there, was field for a holy harvest. Above its two thousand housetops rose the slate-blue steeples of thirty-one
churches and forty-five abbeys, priories, monasteries, and convents—not to mention the private chapels and countless ora-
tories of noble houses in which Mass was offered every day
or the flèche of Saint Denis-du-Pas, the former pro-cathedral,
now somewhat overwhelmed by the enormous cathedral of
Notre Dame. A hum of dedication, like the sound of locusts
on a hot day in Provence, arose regularly at devotional hours
from this forest of crosses.

The mass of buildings, crowded within ramparts, was also
a forest of magnificent turrets, lodges, watchtowers, and plat-
forms, for the architects of the time, with extraordinary lack
of parsimony, had designed each defense construction to be
an ornament as well. Seven turreted entrances on the right
bank and seven on the left, each beautifully and finely
wrought, opened into the fortifications of the city. Each man-
sion had its own garden, each house its own device, each
church its own graveyard. Parisians were cared for in thirty
hospitals and supplied from eleven public markets. The Tour

de Nesle and the Tour Barbeau surveyed all river navigation, ready to block passage if necessary by a chain barricade. Outside the city, ten *faubourgs*, each a village in itself, clustered near to the exterior abbeys—and to the wine presses. In this first quarter of the sixteenth century, when Faith would withstand attack to reappear in its full clarity, when ideas were seeking new channels and art new forms of expression, Paris was already a great urban center.

Francis Xavier reached the left bank of the city on the Feast of Saint Remigius as the autumn leaves were falling. He saw the gentle movement of a hundred masts in the port of the river Seine, and beyond them a great mass of fine dwellings, each more beautiful than the other. Across from him rose the thick, cone-shaped tower of the Louvre, where the King had decided to establish residence. On the left bank lay his immediate destination, the University quarter.

This Latin Quarter, or "Latin country" as it was called, consisted of a group of sixty colleges in a labyrinth of lanes and narrow passageways, on the eastern slope of the Mont Sainte Geneviève. Most of these colleges, which comprised some four thousand students of every nationality, were installed in the town house of some illustrious *seigneur*, purchased from him and subsidized by a specific prince or city— hence the names: College of Beauvais, of Lisieux, of Le Mans, of Reims.

The University was a republic of professors—a federate republic of seven companies, each with its individual government. Three of these were comprised of the masters in theology, canon law, and medicine—all faculties of superior reputation. In the inferior faculty of arts, however, which included the full teaching group of the colleges, the masters were more numerous by far, forming four companies called the "nations": the nation of Normandy; the nation of Picardy; Germany, for all foreigners of Germanic idiom, including English and Scotch; France, for the provinces to the east, west, and south of Paris and for foreigners from the southern states.

The faculties of law and medicine, being fairly recent, were not yet firmly established, and teaching was done outside the college in the house of the professors or "regents." In each college, instruction was for the group as such, so that the University included a great number of regents, some having no more than twenty-five student-disciples. Each class was an open discussion in which none ran the risk of being left to himself. Keen competitions and rivalries were unavoidable in this closed system, which could cast doubt on such and such a master, or give rise to contempt and mutual distrust within the fervent and unseeing ranks. Regents and students moved in a body, their nightly outings leading to occasional rioting in the same streets where, not a hundred years before, the student-vagabond François Villon had made sport of waking up good folk with some genial discourtesy.

The Latin Quarter of today remains unchanged. The same narrow passageways entwine the same academic walls; and in the *bistros*, the same wine animates the same discussions. There are no two ways of being young.

Francis found himself in an impassioned city. Christian unity no longer existed, and the word "freedom" was spoken with a note of defiance that has since become familiar. Little by little the Renaissance, profoundly unjust at first in its spirit of rejection, was finding its truth and its harmonies. Rocks appeared in the tranquil channels of tradition. There were sudden upsets. Many were wounded in the sounding destruction of aged vessels manned by overconfident pilots; but their freight was no longer of value. The pathetic Middle Ages, having died a protracted death for over two hundred years, was repudiated by those discovering a sense of evolution. In France, the French language was coming into its own.

The date 1525 marks an extraordinary year in the history of Paris. Never has youth felt so keenly that nothing in the future should rely on a framework of the past. All would be a new beginning. Never has the conflict between generations been so painful. Teachers cast off their academic hoods, asking to return to their studies; outstandingly gifted students were thrust suddenly into a professorial chair. In the general madness—and under the chill ironic glance of that rasping ancestor of Voltaire, Desiderius Erasmus—a world was dying. The older generation, depressed and without courage, could only decry all new ideas.

Francis was caught up in the rising surge of the new current. Portuguese comrades drew him to the College of Sainte-Barbe, owned by one Diogo de Gouvea and under the illustrious protection of the King of Portugal. The College consisted of seven buildings dispersed through an ample park and separated by an irregular pattern of fences and masonry from the rival College of Montaigu, outstanding in its teaching and terrifying in its austerity. The block of Sainte-Barbe, still recognizable today, was enclosed at either end by the rue des Sept Voies and the rue des Cholets; on the two sides, by the rue des Chiens and the rue de Reims.

No one knows the exact location of Francis' room, the *turne* he shared with three comrades from the south and later with Favre and Loyola. We know only that he kept the room for eleven years, well after his studies had been completed. It may perhaps have been reached through a spiral stairway worked into one of the turrets adorning the exterior façade of the building.

For the moment, sensing nothing of a future vocation, Francis devoted himself to study. For the next eight years, sharing the exaltations of other students, he would discuss, affirm, laugh, argue, and wax eloquent. Life was rigorous at Sainte-Barbe. A youth of nineteen, Henri de Mesmes, the youngest to receive a University doctorate, writes of the time:

We were up at four A.M., and having said our prayers, trailed an hour later to the hall of studies, with our big books under our arms and our inkpots and candlesticks in our hands. There was no break in the lessons until ten o'clock, when we were given something to eat. After dinner, by way of recreation, we read Sophocles, Aristophanes, or Euripides, and sometimes Demosthenes, Cicero, Vergil, and Horace. At one o'clock we began private study. We had supper at six o'clock and then read more Greek or Latin.[1]

The basis of the program was Aristotelian philosophy, from which one might attain to all domains of knowledge or speculation. At no point was the subject matter scientific or positive. It led, on the contrary, to an ever more penetrating meditation on life and on mankind, with the constant risk of exceeding limits imposed by doctoral wisdom on the development of thought. The Church, fearing youth's natural penchant for intellectual hazards, kept close watch over the regents. In dogma alone lay the measure of order, of prudence, even of respect—a stern measure for the emancipated and ardent "barbistes."

It is doubtful, however, that Francis Xavier ever followed a schedule like that of the youthful Doctor de Mesmes. His mind—alert, inquiring, interested—understood without difficulty; he was neither slow nor brilliant. Perhaps he lacked the patience and the inclination to construct a slow pyramid of arguments which would in the long run yield but an indefinite picture of man. Perhaps, too, without knowing where or by whom, he felt himself called, and was instinctively preparing for the immense solitude of the future by living intensely the life of the city around him.

Sainte-Barbe's extensive grounds lay not far from the gardens of the Abbey Sainte Geneviève, within a few yards of the city wall and open countryside. But for the time being, Francis, knowing the tedium of the country, preferred the congested rue des Chiens and the narrow streets of the Latin Quarter. Moreover, he was a frequent participant in the sports activities of Ile Notre Dame, where, according to Loyola, he was "one of the finest high-jumpers on the island."

Bordered by willows and poplar trees, Ile Notre Dame belonged to the chapter of the metropolitan church. In 1360 a channel had been cut, forming the small Ile aux Vaches at the far end of Ile Notre Dame. Beyond lay the enchanting Ile Louviers, whose groves and manorland served as a practice ground for crossbowmen. An extraordinary sight, that of the broad river busy with ships, its wooded isles forming an extension of the great, burdened Ile de la Cité. On busy days, small craft bringing hay from Port Saint Paul would find a mooring among the islands. There were water festivals, and on Ile Notre Dame a refreshment stand established by the chapter proved more than popular. The red wine of Montrouge flowed generously, the white wine of Vaugirard, the rosé of Saint-Marceau . . . Washerwomen came by boat each morning—singing, spreading their wet linen on the grass to bleach, doubtless raising their heads to follow the student games.

Francis reached the island by crossing the footbridge of La Tournelle. Bow and robe were carried by his valet—for this young gentleman's son, minding not the ruin of Xavier, had a non-resident valet, one Miguel Landivar, a crafty and dangerous organizer of artful combines. Francis, in the manner of all youth, was impatient to "live." He had decided that his life should be without mediocrity, and, if possible, without boredom. His allocation of family money was quickly spent. He borrowed. "Appearance"—for he was proud of his birth—

was important. He must have a good horse and fine garments. Charming, he charmed all, feeling no urge to overexertion in the heady ease of Paris ways.

No figure is more appealing than this proud, exuberant, receptive youth, whose studies neither weakened his eyes nor deformed his back, whose amusements were not a waste of time, whose laugh gave no offense. Impertinent but generous, Francis passed from one mood to another without for a moment breaking faith with himself or with his friends. Later on, drawing pagans to God and converting ignorant souls, he would succeed less by dialectics than by charm, by the tremendous impact of his personality. Francis was not a master in theology, but he was a master in love. In Asia, he would be surrounded by children . . .

On October 1, 1526, he began his studies in philosophy. Sainte-Barbe was troubled by a division of thought between regents and principal. Diogo de Gouvea, a staunch Catholic and second Dean of the Faculty of Theology, had issued directives intended, if possible, to check the influence of Luther in the University. A docile and conforming son of the Church, too positive to doubt and too old to oppose established ideas, he had nevertheless been unable to restrain several of Sainte-Barbe's regents from being receptive to the new "humanism" and consequently to certain basic principles of the Reformation. The Church was changing—or at least lacking its former strength and solidity. Dogmas were to be re-examined. Rome was thinking of Trent. The new critical spirit of the humanists invited opposition to certain immutable laws, displeasing to the young precisely because they were immutable; and professors at Sainte-Barbe led their students much further than Diogo de Gouvea would have wished.

In this Paris where Francis had now been living for a year, the temperature was rising. A statue of the Virgin was destroyed at night by agitating "extremists." The King ordered a new one cast in solid silver and came in person to the Latin Quarter for its installation. On other less justifiable occasions, however—and in truth, against the will of the King and despite the pacific intervention of his sister, Marguerite de Valois—students were "invited" to the St. John's fires in the Place de Grève where they witnessed the burning of those who had disseminated the new ideas. Marguerite was more than inclined to shelter early supporters of the Reformation; and Francis I, who at thirty-two had a marked predilection for intrepid thinking, protected the "Evangélistes," including them in his passionate sympathy for the humanists.[2]

In 1527, through her marriage with Henri d'Albret, Marguerite became Queen of Navarre. Throughout their lifetime, she and her husband dreamed of reconstituting the Navarre of Juan de Jassu. Francis Xavier must have had a liking for his young queen, and could not have been quick to reject the ideas she was so ready to affirm. It is highly probable that he lent himself to the new critical spirit, listening by night in the shadowy streets or in some recessed garden spot to the agents of innovation—perhaps to Calvin himself, about whom centered many clandestine gatherings within the colleges. Yet Francis must have felt something of the real difficulty which the issue was creating for other consciences; and in this respect there must have been incidents which wounded him. He was to become—and not much later—totally opposed to the evangelism of pre-reformists and completely unbelieving of their ideas.

III

At four in the morning—and one can imagine, in that closely inhabited quarter, the flowering of lighted tapers behind thick walls—a student-philosopher, qualified as the public "rouser," made the rounds of all rooms in the college to importune those whose eyes did not open with the required speed. He supplied a light "when the season required," although one may suppose that at that hour within the narrow apertures of the aged Hôtel de Chalon light was always "required." At five, all students were seated on the floor of their respective classrooms—straw was supplied only for examination days—and the regents began a first hour of lessons. After that all went to the chapel and then for something to eat. This was taken at leisure during a period of relaxation lasting until eight which was not supposed to become a recreation. From eight until ten came the major class of the morning, prolonged until eleven by individual supervised work. At eleven, masters and students repaired together to the refectory, where a meal was served in the presence of the principal, who followed the chaplain's final grace with divers brief observations on the conduct of the college. When necessity commanded, he might upbraid a poor student, since public physical humiliation was held salutary for the character of even the oldest. Inigo de Loyola, as a Navarrese nobleman well known for his travels and for the unique fervor of his faith, would be so threatened at the age of thirty-eight.

At the regents' table in the refectory sat Jean Penna, Francis
Xavier's professor of philosophy and the dominating figure
of the college, as well as Mathurin Cordier, who was charged
with the "young," for whose benefit he wished to initiate
French instead of Latin as the language for rudimentary lessons. There was Strébée, who had started out washing corri-
dors as a domestic and who rose to become the most elegant
Latinist of his time. There was the impetuous Spaniard
Gelida, master of Latin and Greek, who prepared his courses
with the help of an extraordinary servant, William Postel, who
was later to establish the teaching of oriental languages. There
was Fernel, whose public lectures in philosophy and mathe-
matics were so popular that his chair had to be drawn out
into the courtyard; and, after 1528, the Scot, Buchanan, who
introduced the "barbistes" to the art of the Renaissance.

In the afternoon, following a brief interrogation on the
morning's lessons, came an hour of free time; from three until
five, a second interrogation—and, finally, supper, Benediction
in the chapel, and bed. Curfew was at nine, but an authorized
candle might burn until eleven. Each one must sleep in his
own quarters and could leave the college only if accompanied
by a surveillant.

Such were the regulations, but they were not rigorously ap-
plied. Francis was doubtless a *portionniste*, or boarder, and
as such did not have the privilege of going and coming at
will. A boarder was better off than a scholarship student;
yet to be a portionniste, no matter how honorable, in this
modest academic hierarchy, implied precise obligations and
in particular a minimum of submission. But Francis was no
longer of an age to be held thus in check. To impress fellows
and influence masters, he urgently requested that attestations
of his noble birth be sent from home. The name of Xavier
carried weight in the now-Spanish Navarre, but not so in

Paris, where proof was required of an established lineage and illustrious name. His family, however, turned a deaf ear to these requests. The young man's escapades were disquieting. He spent too much money, and in suspect company. Moreover, he was too sure of himself.

He could think himself settled at Sainte-Barbe for a considerable period of time. After the six or seven years required for the master of arts, there was a possibility of continuing for thirteen years more to obtain a doctorate in theology. But destiny was to destroy this patient, two-decade project, which, when he was forty, might have assured Francis a fine bishopric. At the end of the rue des Sept Voies, he could glimpse the cathedral of Notre Dame; in the other direction lay Sainte-Geneviève. Throughout the entire Latin Quarter, each street, each alleyway, each little square had its own shrine. Impossible not to think of God. Impossible to imagine a glory not of God. Christianity might lie in the hollow of a wave, but the Cross would not go down. Feeling this, Francis knew that what he wanted was responsibility in the administration of the Church. He was clearly not humble. God's service requires tremendous strength of soul, a prodigious will to act. Francis had grace and stature, a desire to command. He perhaps foresaw that the Church needed leaders and that he was born to lead.

For some time he had been sharing his room with Pierre Favre, a broad-shouldered Savoyard whose extraordinary learning included Greek and Latin as well as philosophy, and who was hesitating between three apostolates: teaching, medicine, and the priesthood. He had tended sheep, although not for his father, as had Francis. Pierre's family, astounded by the shepherd's intelligence, had made sacrifices to send him to Paris at nineteen. The studious boy, attentive to others and to the workings of Grace within himself, was both poetic and deeply spiritual. Francis liked him. The reticent Favre, however, was not one to impose his faith on another. Without any loss of rapport, each remained firmly entrenched in his own attitude. Favre stayed close to his books and to his work of planning out Penna's lectures. His was the candle to burn late while Francis, loosing his horse, rode here and there through the city. Yet in divine knowledge they were perhaps equal . . . Francis, neither a scholar nor a theologian, was a "leader of men" in whom matters of general culture would be surpassed by depth of character and strong nerves.

The licentiate—an authorization to teach—was obtained after formal examination in transcendant logic, dialectics, metaphysics, geometry, and astronomy. There were two sessions, one of which was public. The other, private and much more severe, took place in the presence of the chancellor at Notre Dame or Sainte-Geneviève. In 1530, five years after his arrival in Paris, Francis Xavier appeared before a chancellor and four examiners; and several days later, in the church of his chancellor, received the apostolic benediction and the right to teach *hic et ubique terrarum*. Such an authorization, however, was purely nominal until one had paid a heavy fee to register with the corporation of masters. If two years elapsed between the granting of Francis' licentiate and his appointment as regent to the College of Dormans-Beauvais, the time was doubtless spent in acquiring the full sum and in working off his brief commitment to the college where he had been a student.

At Sainte-Barbe, where Francis continued to live, his things had been pushed aside to make room for a new companion, Inigo de Loyola, who arrived in 1529. Between Francis and Inigo, sympathy was impossible. Everything held them apart. Francis was in his twenties; Inigo nearly forty. Francis was tall and athletic; Inigo short, and, since his wound at Pamplona, awkward. Francis was outgoing and excitable; Inigo looked on, grave and self-possessed. Francis made use of his name; Inigo said nothing. Finally, the Xavier family had fought for a French Navarre, and Inigo had been of the opposition. This fair and graying nobleman, recommended by the archbishop of Toledo, was a famous captain and an astonishing mystic—a personality both to be feared and treated with respect. His conversion had come at Loyola, in a room to which he had been transported after the many operations necessitated by his serious wound. There, forced meditation, a book on the lives of saints, had brought this arrogant aristocrat to a serious self-examination and inspired the ebullient and dashing cavalier with the idea of combat for Christ rather than for a prince of the world. As soon as he was able, Inigo made a retreat at Montserrat, stripping himself of his fine garments and laying down sword and dagger at the feet of the Madonna. In rope shoes and sackcloth he mingled with the crowd of pilgrims, with whom, at two in the morning, in the clear starlight of a March night, he received Holy Communion for the first time.

Although he planned to spend but one night at Manresa, which was near Montserrat, he remained a year. There, all was weighed, experienced, understood . . . then came Rome, Venice, Jaffa, where the humble tourist was beset by brigands, pursued by pirates, even taken for a spy. At long last, however, the idea of the priesthood was growing on him. He was over thirty when he began studies at Barcelona, where, two years later, he received a diploma qualifying him to study physics and theology at the University of Alcala. There, the curious and compelling student alarmed the Inquisition, and after forty-two days in prison, Inigo set out for Salamanca. Lack of discretion, however, brought him once again to imprisonment and chains. Outraged, he left once more—this time for Paris.

Inigo presented himself as a non-resident at Montaigu, taking lodging at the Hospice of Saint James in the remote rue Saint Denis. The unkempt student who traveled so far every day was not well received, and when he persuaded two boarders to leave Montaigu for the hospice, there was a general uprising. His position had by now considerably improved thanks to sums of money which correspondents of his family had been keeping for him in Bruges and London, and once more Inigo changed residence. Diogo de Gouvea received him at Sainte-Barbe on condition that there be no more eccentric behavior, and assigned him to the room occupied by Francis and Pierre Favre. The bout was over. God had bound the sheaf: Loyola, Favre, and Xavier—unsuspecting founders of the Society of Jesus.

Favre was delighted by the newcomer's arrival; Francis, less than pleased. Inigo plunged into his studies, and Diogo de Gouvea asked Francis to help him with special lessons. The new licentiate quickly handed over this task to a willing Favre, and in one corner of the turne, intent whispering could be heard far into the night. Francis would leave the room or survey the two new friends with enmity, although he was nevertheless obliged to share their meal from time to time since it was traditional for students to give small supper parties in their own rooms, where individual conversation could escape the noisy din of the refectory.

It was in Loyola's blood to form groups about himself. He had already made two unsuccessful attempts: a little group organized at Barcelona had followed him to Alcala and Salamanca, only to dissolve at the departure of its leader for Paris; the second attempt had succeeded in wresting three Spanish students from the Latin Quarter for a few days only. This time would finally bring results. The three men in the turne at Sainte-Barbe constituted a small association—one as yet unconsolidated but whose growth would know no limits. They could not foresee that the total membership would one day stand at thirty-three thousand.[3]

Favre, after considerable indecision, had determined on the priesthood. By intensive "cramming," he had received the bachelor's degree in January 1529, and the licentiate at Easter. His new knowledge, up to this point drawn only from books, was shared with Inigo, who, in turn, spoke of his travels, his discussions, his meditations—of Manresa. The learning of one and the life experience of the other combined to shape their inspiration and their friendship. Francis was far from sympathetic and was not amused. Favre had abandoned him for this new companion; his room, with their discussions, devotions, and late-burning candles, was no longer his own. Nor would Inigo keep to his own affairs. He lost no chance to engage Francis in conversation and showed a sympathetic interest which nothing could discourage, even to lending him money . . .

It is extraordinary that Francis could maintain this unfavorable impression during five years of sharing a room with Inigo—five years without understanding and without tolerance. The two, whose similar genius would eventually be drawn into a deep and lasting friendship, were constantly at odds. "I once heard it said by our great shaper of souls," wrote Juan Polanco, Loyola's secretary, "that the toughest dough he ever kneaded was, at the start, the young Francis Xavier, whom God has used, nevertheless, more than any other subject of our time." But Francis' antipathy was not strong enough for him to seek a change of quarters. Apparently, his youthful ardor was not yet ready to give up those things that Inigo found superfluous: sports, horses, velvet cloaks. After all, Inigo, at Francis' age, had owned such things and known such pleasures . . .

In 1532 Francis was named professor of philosophy at the College of Dormans-Beauvais. He was twenty-six and pleased with life. From now on he would be more independent, speaking from a professorial chair, and slipping in among Aristotle's ideas an occasional thought of his own, seeing, perhaps, an answering gleam in the youthful eyes fixed on him—in the restless, vacant eyes of those whose age was just what his had been when he first arrived from Navarre.

IV

Francis' instruction at Dormans, for all his fiery talent, may not have been particularly brilliant. He was neither a rhetorician nor, strictly speaking, an intellectual; and his knowledge of Latin was inadequate to deal with the subtleties of philosophic reasoning. When his following proved sparse, Inigo sought zealously to recruit paying students—acting perhaps out of friendship, perhaps out of respect for the ardent gifts of the young professor. As regent or missionary, Francis would be consistently gay and forthright. "In any conversation, keep a gay and pleasant face," he writes, "nothing sorry, nothing sad."[4]

At Dormans he met the youthful humanist Pierre Ramus, well versed in all fields even as an adolescent, and ready perhaps to communicate his disdainful conclusions on the genius of Aristotle, whom he made bold to contest. There, too, Francis had as a student one Nicolas Bobadilla—a difficult, complex, and violently individualistic character, who was to become his disciple and would one day share in his great venture.

When his plan of courses had been established, Francis finally registered in the faculty of theology, doubtless having been invited to do so by Diogo de Gouvea, one of its outstanding figures.

Francis' new activities were making him known, and the

attestation of noble birth became increasingly important. But Maria Azpicuelta was no longer living, and the men of Xavier had no time for their turbulent younger brother.

In the shaded park of the Carthusians, at a spot where today the Avenue de l'Observatoire crosses the rue Cassini, Loyola, Favre, and Francis were walking on a Sunday afternoon. Francis kept a little to one side, breathing in the smell of earth under the great trees. In eight years he had come to know every street of the "Latin country," all its exaltations—and joy, with that which makes joy die away. Now, in the shadowy *allées* away from the din, he pondered, wondering. He held the master of arts from the University—no mean honor at a moment when the University area covered one third of Paris, and when the members of this great body, the most important in the State, constituted in themselves a quasi-nobility subject to no law. Yet with every reason to be happy, he was not. Francis Xavier—Navarrese nobleman and Parisian dignitary—was dissatisfied. Sports on the island were less amusing. Gay company was less desirable, especially since a professor, in dedication to his calling, should remain unwed. Francis had not gone this year, as was his habit, to witness the brutal lighting of the Saint John's fires on the Place de Grève. He no longer spent his evenings at a wooden table in the open street, drinking deep draughts of good, free-flowing Parisian wine. Deep within him there stirred an inexplicable unrest, an expectant hope. He was standing before a door unevenly joined, through whose apertures came fine shafts of light. Beyond lay the sun—but where was beyond?

In the Carthusian garden, a young man is lost in thought. Not far away, two men are waiting.

V

It has been said that Francis Xavier was no lover of nature; and in truth his letters never dwell on the burnished gold of Asia that has proved so captivating to others. His soul and his imagination envisioned other landscapes, infinite in perspective; yet his gay, well-ordered character, loving the limpid, the pleasant, the tender, was certainly drawn to things which time did not permit him to describe. He liked the Carthusian garden as a place to breathe and meditate. The park was for Francis what Manresa had been for Inigo—a withdrawal, a re-evaluation, God's secret conquest of a youthful reserve . . .

The years together at Sainte-Barbe had not reconciled Francis and Inigo, but now, driven from the stifling rue des Chiens to spend their Sundays in the property of the good Fathers, they talked more openly and with a calm serenity as the milder air of the faubourg carried, leafwise, from one to the other a truth that was theirs to share.

Francis was subject to many pressures. The University was fiercely conservative, while the Court, counterbalancing Church, University, and Parliament, was humanistic. He was clearly sympathetic to the intelligent sovereign respected by his brothers Miguel and Juan; and to the charming Marguerite of dissevered Navarre. For the younger generation, traditional disciplines were being undermined. They had thought only of Heaven; now happiness was to be of the earth. A modest fleet of caravels had destroyed notions accepted as articles of faith. An increase in private wealth and the rediscovery of the past meant new ways of living and new breadth for intellectual horizons. In the currents and eddies of reform, none might float uncommitted. The spirit of reformation could not fail to appeal to a young man of twenty-seven eager for intellectual adventure. Politically, it was not without anarchy, thanks to an overzealous avant-garde whose indiscretions were beginning to try the patience of the protector-king. Without being particularly pious, Francis reflected on the problems of the Church he was to serve and saw it not only menaced, but unsettled. The institution within which he hoped to become a leader and a prince was in danger. His pride could not conceive of accepting rank in a weakened hierarchy, or of rallying the new Church in a spirit of romantic subterfuge that would negate his childhood.

The decision was made. No longer, on his way from Sainte-Barbe to Dormans, would he stop to visit with the erudite printer-scholar Robert Estienne, whose press faced the Chapelle Saint-Jean. Francis had done this fairly often, for the extraordinary Estiennes were hospitable and their house a brilliant circle where one might play with the fire of the new ideas. There he had perhaps encountered the King and Queen, faithful friends of Estienne who came purely to watch him at work and who might sit quietly in a corner as he corrected proof . . .

The Estienne family was Provençal in origin, former lords of the picturesque town of Lambesc. At the time of Francis' appointment to Dormans, young Robert, with his learned child-wife, had just published a monumental Bible in Latin. It was drawn up according to the Saint Jerome version with a summary before each chapter, a detailed concordance in the margin, variants referring to the Hebrew text, and, at the end, a voluminous index giving names of persons, cities, rivers, and mountains in Hebrew, Chaldean, Greek, and Latin. The immense work, bearing the seal of the King's approval, had meant years of research in the royal library and in the abbeys of Saint Germain des Prés and Saint Denis, and had acquired immediate fame. The Church, however, despite its initial interest, had discouraged and finally condemned all distribution of the work.

Enough, then, of Estienne and his friends. Francis had made a definite choice in the Church of Clement VII, which was sufficiently tolerant and persuasive to bring fruitful results from a meeting at Marseilles between the Pope and the King of France. Nothing was stable, including, of course, the Church, but that institution in the long run gave no serious indications of total collapse. The Bishop of Paris was an intellectual, a collector of books and manuscripts, a man open to suggestion. Such an authority could impart confidence to a young regent anxious to be obedient while maintaining his critical spirit. If, moreover, one single landmark could be said to dominate the Latin Quarter, occupying its summit and visible from afar, it was the belltower of Sainte-Geneviève . . . Francis Xavier, son of the Church, had resolved the first crisis of his life.

But there remained yet another. Favre, now an ordained priest, had departed to spend seven months with his father in Savoie. Francis was left at Sainte-Barbe to share the turne with Inigo, who had been sent before Diogo de Gouvea, accused by the philosopher Penna of "undirected mysticism" —a strong accusation in such excessive times. The fact that he had emerged from the interview arm in arm with the principal had escaped no one and aroused much admiring comment.

Imperceptibly at first, then suddenly, Francis capitulated to Inigo—and through Inigo, to God. The conversion had many implications. He would renounce every title and privilege. He would turn aside from the course he had pursued for eight years. At an age when reason tempers a thirst for the unknown, he would take the plunge, as had Inigo. The latter, too, had known an ambitious youth and the pride of a famous name. He, too, had been touched by Grace and scarred in the encounter. But example does not explain all. Deeply shaken, Francis sought to give up his position at Dormans, the room at Sainte-Barbe, his entire wardrobe. Inigo, who had proved that the extraordinary leads to disorder, discouraged this. Francis must change nothing in his way of life. He must wait —and waiting, for him, was a real ordeal, as Inigo knew.

Francis and Favre, flanking Inigo, were now a familiar sight in the Carthusian garden—the "Iniguistas," as they were called until Loyola, annoyed, changed his name to "Ignace" in the French manner. They were joyous, approachable, in the faith that had come to them as a hidden but powerful morning wind, cleaning the atmosphere of mists and removing from their young hearts what there remained of doubt and fear and vanity. Francis' conversion was an established fact. Such spiritual reversals are not unusual; the wonder is not that this occurs, but that it never fails. Such is the Christian miracle. Yet all are not so touched. Landivar, Francis' valet, embittered at losing a lavish and high-living master, lay in wait in a corridor to deal Loyola a mortal blow—but in vain. Loyola was not scratched. With this minor drama Francis' second crisis was passed. No forbidding frown marked his features, but rather a radiant enthusiasm neither austere nor immoderate. He was simply at peace.

Ignatius proved extremely conservative at the start of his

new leadership, with no desire to attract fresh blame or persecution by having the little group make itself conspicuous. Each man was to maintain his work, fulfill all regular duties, and continue to see his friends. Meetings would be secret, away from any hostile ear. Soon they were joined by the exuberant student from Dormans, Nicolas de Bobadilla, and then by a second difficult individualist, Simon Rodriguez—a phlegmatic young gentleman not averse to fame and glory, who was at the moment studying at Sainte-Barbe with funds from his suzerain, the King of Portugal. And there were two others—young students of theology from Alcala who had, on their arrival, entrusted themselves to Ignatius and formed a close friendship. One was Diego Laynez, aged twenty-two, of Jewish parentage, who was to become a major figure in the debates of the Council of Trent and, later, the second general of the Jesuits. The younger, Alfonso Salmeron, was nineteen. The seven, drawn together in a common foresight and anticipating their as yet undeveloped gifts, included even then four Jesuits famous in history: Loyola, Favre, Xavier, and Laynez.

Ignatius pondered. He had formed a group, but to what purpose? The answer need not be hurried. One by one—and in his own case, with difficulty—each received the master of arts degree. At a time when censorship and ill will existed even within the Church itself, they must not be criticized for lack of intellectual grounding. He knew, however, that Paris was no field for their activity, for it offered nothing new or important to be accomplished. It was not an unhappy city, and provision had been made for all works of charity, but to serve the bishopric of Paris meant to disappear into a vast whole, each man going his separate way according to the positions to be filled. They must initiate a separate order.

The question would be under consideration for several

years. Only one decision had been taken, that of being a group apart, responsible to papal authority alone. They conceived their mission as a form of chivalry—a concept not too astonishing when four of them had actually been brought up as knights, hearing family legends told at family firesides and viewing any enterprise from a predetermined angle, with God, first and foremost, the King of Heaven. Their solemn pledge would also be inspired by chivalry. Ignatius was the first founder of an order to begin with the ceremony of a secret oath, combining childlike fervor with a taste for courtly ritual which recalled the poems of old.

Separation from the Latin Quarter was essential. Only apart from familiar surroundings could one feel oneself "available," and so for the oath he chose to lead them up the Butte Montmartre to a remote chapel on a lonely road, in a bleak and rocky landscape not far from the well-known abbey of the Benedictines. The chapel, called the *Martyrium*, had been built in the ninth century on the site of a quarry which had held the relics of Christian martyrs. It was there, according to tradition, that Saint Denis had been beheaded; and it was there, in 1392, that Charles VI had prayed to regain his reason while his queen, Isabeau, instructed her pages, who were disguised as little devils, to rush in on him. Rebuilt in 1134, the Martyrium was now in partial ruins and consisted of a simple chapel with a crypt reached by a flight of fifteen steps. Ordinarily it was kept closed.

On the morning of August 15, 1534, Ignatius and his companions knocked at the door of the abbey and, because Favre was a priest, they were given the key. Through the heat and the buzzing flies, the Iniguistas—Loyola, Xavier, Bobadilla, Rodriguez, Laynez, and Salmeron—descended into the crypt after Favre, who celebrated the Mass. Before the Communion each of the seven solemnly pledged "poverty and chastity; to

set out for Jerusalem; and upon return to consecrate (himself) with God's help to the salvation of infidels as well as of
the faithful."[5] To this, they added their pledge to meet yearly
in the crypt on the same date. After the ceremony, they left
the chapel and, gathering branches to make a fire, ate their
meal on the hillside with practical simplicity. No morbid
austerity was to complicate their joy or close their hearts, but
Ignatius, older and responsible for their commitment, knew
that the day would have far-reaching consequences[6] . . .

Francis went back to his teaching at Dormans—perhaps
with new zeal, with a bit of the fire that had entered his life;
perhaps bringing to his dialectics the zest of an inner fervor.
In any case, Diogo de Gouvea, informed of what had taken
place, could dismiss any previous doubts about Francis and
congratulate himself on having disregarded advice not to place
his confidence in Ignatius. He, too, felt the group should not
be Church-attached and set about finding an appropriate
channel.

Towards the end of September, Francis left for a month's
retreat—his first—under the direction of Ignatius. Their destination was unknown—perhaps Montmartre or the Carthusian
garden, or some more remote location. We know only that
Ignatius was present to visit and advise.

During this retreat, Francis subjected himself to rigorous
fast and mortification, his body so tightly bound with cords
that at one point amputation of his badly swollen arm seemed
almost necessary. "But," writes Simon Rodriguez, "after caus-
ing him two days of frightful suffering, the cord burst. By
the singular mercy of God, and in a manner beyond . . . com-
prehension, he was suddenly restored to health." This mortification was hardly typical of Francis, who had never believed
self-imposed suffering was necessarily pleasing to God. To
weaken oneself unnaturally is, on the contrary, to destroy in

part a strength given for God's service. The body bears for a time a human soul. To misuse it unreasonably is to be a poor workman, in danger of injuring a share of eternal treasure and of overestimating the flesh while claiming to bring it to terms. This, Ignatius recalled severely to Francis, who answered that as one entering on the way of renunciation, he had wished to see how much physical discomfort his mind could endure without losing its freedom. As a young man who would subject himself, among other things, to the discipline of chastity, he had found the experiment rewarding, but he did not believe, at this time or any other, that mortification was necessary in itself, or even particularly noteworthy. Not being an ascetic, he perhaps saw it as a source of healthy fatigue, replacing the sports to which he had once been so devoted.

Ignatius put Francis to the test of the *Spiritual Exercises*, his original technique of thought direction which draws souls to a high point of fervor. It is a skillful system of self-examination and persuasion which can loose the tangled skein of self, discipline the imagination, and hold an individual up to his most lofty capabilities. Divided into thirty "days," the exercises exact perfect obedience. The "director" charged with their application establishes a program by which the new disciple must meditate hour by hour on a given thought or contemplate a given scene, the whole forming a disciplined, organized progression of interior "slide projections." A picture is "shown" and described by the director, contemplated by the disciple, then followed by another picture. The initiate has the difficult obligation of creating, on command and without exterior inspiration, specific images within himself. Few men are capable of this in themselves. Loyola therefore

. . . subjects the imagination to a methodical training: the disciple must first picture a given scene to himself in a convincing manner, next people it with clearly delineated characters; and finally, if necessary, supply a dramatic element endowing the characters with speech and action. Ignatius warns meanwhile against dwelling over the composition of each tableau. The *Exercises* must focus our human imagination, so easily misleading, on an evocative picture which may in turn summon up a determination of the will. With this intent, he not only chooses them carefully, but seeks in each preparatory prayer to awaken a particular emotion which can be developed by the nature of the exercise itself. All of this reveals a masterful direction of souls and a profound knowledge of the human heart which are worthy of the highest admiration.[7]

Francis was transported. If his life was henceforth free from doubt, the fact can perhaps be attributed to this first retreat, this probation which taught him above all else the importance of self-mastery, the need for a character without breach or blemish and impervious to doubt or heresy.

The Iniguistas, without further hesitation, had embraced the conservative cause as guardians of the Faith. They became trees whose stout roots could prevent a landslide, the head battalion of an army to combat heresy and idolatry— a battalion whose fervor would compel the admiration of even those whom it most vigorously opposed. Francis Xavier, after Francis of Assisi, became the preferred saint of Protestantism.

Ignatius' aim was to restore to the Western Church the power it had known in the thirteenth century when the Capetian monarchy was united with the Holy See. Was not the Marseilles meeting in 1533 reminiscent of such a rapport? The thirteenth century had seen two new orders, Franciscans and Dominicans, bring preachers and missionaries and new depths of mysticism to the magnificent monastic flowering of the previous era. The order of which Ignatius was now thinking

would mean another spring season for the Church. Philosophy, in the thirteenth century, had waited on theology, and
he was determined not to permit its escape from the theologic
mold. All was propitious, though pressing. He had come at
the right time.

"Human society," writes a Protestant historian of the nineteenth century, "in order to live and develop, has need of two
things: liberty and regulation—a nice adjustment between elements of stability and those of change."[8] Nor must elements
of "change" such as the sixteenth-century humanists serve to
uproot the Church by their agitations. In this Ignatius saw
his task, and his companions found themselves charged with
establishing an "adjustment" of the various forces pulling on
the Church from all directions. A thrilling mission in its nu-
ance, subtlety, and scope—and remarkably perceived by one
individual during the most splendid days of the Renaissance.

Back again in Paris, Francis wrote to his brother, Juan de
Jassu, head of the family since the premature death of Miguel.
Juan had made a wealthy marriage and was living a life of
lordly idleness in the castle of Obanos near Pamplona. Xavier
and some of its land might at that moment have been recovered, but such was not Francis' intention. He does not,
however, conceal the fact that, despite his vow of poverty, a
few *cruzados* might not be inappropriate:

In your comfortable home you have been fully apprised of my
poverty and of the daily difficulties that I encounter here in Paris,
where I am lacking in everything. My needs arise from the fact
that Your Grace is not entirely aware of my difficulties. I suffer
them in the certain hope that Your Grace, convinced, by careful
investigation, of my misery, will generously be willing to put an
end to it.

"Apprised," "aware"—an obvious contradiction. Francis, unable to reclaim any part of his inheritance, was clearly hoping for a pension; and the request, no matter what his intention, was fully justified. He was at least entitled to the income from Xavier, which was not Juan's residence.

Who would deliver the letter? Ignatius himself, suffering from an ailment for which his own native air had been advised as treatment, left for Navarre bearing numerous letters for Juan, for the family of Laynez, and that of Salmeron. "There is no indication," writes Father Brodrick, "of how the cold-blooded hero of Navarre received Saint Ignatius, nor whether he parted with a single one of his superabundant *cruzados*."[9] This would have been highly improbable. Loyola's poor reputation had persisted in Spain.

Francis' letter defends him:

Senor, the Reverend Brother Vear, in the course of his recent visit to this University, informed me of certain complaints which Your Grace formulates against me and discussed them with me at some length. If all is true, as he gave me to understand, the fact of your distress is the sign and proof of the great love you bear me. My own exceeding disturbance in this affair comes from the grief occasioned Your Grace by the idle talk of those evil and despicable men. I wish to identify the lot and pay them their due. Since I number only friends here, it is difficult for me to know what is involved. God knows what it costs me that I must needs put off the punishment they deserve. My only consolation is in the thought that an affair deferred is not abandoned.

That Your Honor may clearly know of the great favor given me by Our Lord in the acquaintance with Senor Maestro Inigo, I hereby give you my word that never will it be possible for me to repay my full debt to him, who has often helped me with money and friends and caused my separation from bad company, which, in my inexperience, I had not recognized to be such. The heresy of

Paris being now revealed, I would not for anything in the world have been associated with its supporters. For this reason alone I owe Inigo a debt impossible to repay—that he kept me from persons full of heresies, while their behavior was above reproach. I therefore beg Your Honor to receive this man, in whose great debt I am, as you would myself. I earnestly beg you to consult with him and to hear his opinion. Believe me, his counsel will profit you greatly, for he is a man of God. I beg Your Grace so to do.

As for all he will say to you of me, grant him the recognition that would be mine if we were speaking together. You will learn from him of my hardships and poverty, for he knows me better than anyone else on earth. If Your Grace wishes to do me the favor of easing my poor state, you may confide to Senor Inigo all that you propose to send me. I finish by kissing the hands of Your Grace and those of the Senora a thousand times. May God grant you a life as long as your noble hearts desire. Your Grace's trusty servant and younger brother Francès de Xavier.[10]

This missive, lacking the beauty of the later messages from Asia, is Francis' one surviving Parisian letter—at best not very adroit. His family had never appreciated the Paris escapade, and his constant requests for money had been poorly received by those to whom, no matter what their subsequent affluence, the year 1515 had brought financial ruin. They knew that their brother had passed his examinations and was a worker. Why, then, had he joined up with a band of visionaries? One might fear the worst. Juan, not a man of learning, was suspicious of Francis; and their sister, the Poor Clare, having died a death of heroic suffering, was no longer there as mediator.

Juan de Jassu, evidently alarmed by Loyola's conversation, consulted the family archives and assembled men of law. Determined in truth to "salvage" his brother, and seeing a means to accomplish it through the vanity he knew so well, he began by arranging a solemn attestation of Francis' noble rank and then secured for him a stall in the chapter of Pamplona. Francis Xavier, chevalier and counsellor to the bishop—this should bring back the lost sheep! Unfortunately, Juan could not foresee the decisions of this new Francis. Our desires at twenty or twenty-five are not what they become as we near thirty, and the arrival in Paris of the long-awaited royal parchment left him unmoved. "We, the Emperor, the Queen, and the King," he read, "affirm and declare by formal and definitive sentence that Don Francisco de Jassu y Xavier is a lord, hidalgo, and gentleman of established lineage. We confer upon him, his sons and direct descendants the right to avail themselves of all prerogatives, exemptions, honors, offices, liberties, privileges, lands, revenues, and dueling rights which are the due of gentlemen, hidalgos, and noblemen in our Kingdom of Navarre and abroad." All very well put but too late. Throughout his life, it is true, Francis would have sharp attacks of pride for being unable to suppress his instincts of home and background. Respectful of the long tradition of the Church, he also respected important families while knowing, nonetheless, that nobility conferred by emperors, queens, and kings could be but ephemeral—God gives more securely, and elsewhere . . .

With his thanks, went his refusal.

On August 15, 1535, all save Ignatius reassembled in the crypt of the Martyrium for the Feast of the Assumption with which the Church honors the Blessed Virgin as a symbol of deepest suffering and transcendant joy. The six companions were thinking with envy of Ignatius. As they pursued ungrateful studies, their leader had outstripped them and was transforming his rest cure into a vigorous spiritual campaign. He had stopped for only a few days at the castle of Loyola, accomplishing his family duties, nevertheless, with due respect. He was gay and natural, out of consideration for parental pride, for Ignatius, like Francis, remained an aristocrat at heart through all his mendicant life, never out of his element while at home, and feeling no guilt for being at ease. Soon, however, he had left the castle and settled in the hospice of Azpeitia—less out of preference for the impoverished than because he could not for a moment forget his solemn vow and chosen mission. A son of Loyola might well pass through castle gates into the intimacy and etiquette of his own home, but the leader of the Iniguistas could not prolong a family interlude. Ignatius consequently cared for the sick and gave instruction to children. Well received by the local clergy, he took advantage of his discussions with worthy priests to arouse in them a more lively faith and a more integrated concept of God's service. This accomplished, he resumed his overland way on foot, visited the parents of his companions, and finally reached Madrid, where the eight-year-old Infanta wished to receive him—an event extraordinary in itself and which, for the "court,"[11] represented a deliberate consecration. Obviously the still obscure "seven," however ill-defined their aims, however doubtful their publicity, had a most compelling leader. Still on foot, Loyola made his way from Madrid to Valencia—a distance of nearly two hundred miles—where, after visiting a Carthusian monk whom he had known in Paris, he embarked for Genoa. New Year's Day, 1537, saw him in Venice.

During the year and a half of Loyola's absence, the group had acquired three additional members who had been approved by Favre: two priests, Le Jay and Broet, and Jean Codure, who for some time had been hovering about. They now numbered ten. Once again, this time with three new initiates, they climbed the Butte Montmartre on August 15. It was 1536—their third Mass at the Martyrium and the second without their founder, whose absence was keenly felt. Ignatius had not thrust them forward to adventure. He had hoped that each would obtain the doctorate in theology even though he himself had renounced it after the master's, since he was neither a scholar nor young enough to relearn, in another form, what he had long since understood. From the heights of Montmartre in the August heat, the wooded hills had the roll of a heavy sea, leading to other inviting worlds beyond. An exaltation seized them—a compulsion to rejoin Ignatius . . .

After the reunion Francis met his classes less frequently. Aristotle seemed arid, yet detachment from Paris was not easy. Eleven years had brought close bonds and friendships. Each man spent two months putting his affairs in order, selling the little he possessed, and saying good-byes. Francis thanked Diogo de Gouvea, paid a farewell visit to the park of the Carthusians, and made his final rounds of the town to which at nineteen he had come one autumn from Navarre. How changed he was and how different the city of Paris, already somewhat transformed in atmosphere by the presence, the activity, the loves of Francis I—whose first love was the city itself.

The nine Iniguistas chose Meaux as their rendezvous, resolving to meet there on December 15, 1536. One by one they took to the road . . .

VI

Nearly thirty miles, with rusty leaves scuffed by walking feet, in a beautiful season but not an easy one . . . Meaux, one of the oldest bishoprics in France, was a good meeting place, for it had known three important councils and the signing of a famous treaty that put an end to the Albigensian war. In Meaux, Catholicity had bested its first opponents—a most reassuring thought for Francis and his friends. There, too, in comparison with Parisian structures, they might see a beautiful cathedral but recently completed. Its flamboyant septipartite rose window cut into the arch above the portal seemed a fit symbol of the fervor radiating within them and cutting deep into their destiny. The rose, however, was dampened by a rain that persisted as far as Metz. Each traveler carried only a small sack containing clean linen, a Bible, and a breviary for that lengthy and curious trip; each wore the robe and bonnet of a Parisian student with a rosary about the neck. There was a daily halt in some small village, where the three priests offered Mass and distributed Communion. They passed themselves off as pilgrims when interrogated by marauding soldiers, and they stopped for supper in hostels where, for lack of funds, they slept in a corner of the common room. Their eastward way led through the Protestant countries, whose major cities, such as Basle, were already won to Luther or Zwingli. The experience was a profitable one, for local pastors, informed of their presence, came to join them at the evening meal in prolonged discussions that were animated without being violent, except at Constance, where rising ill will caused them to take flight.

The bitter cold did not affect their good humor. Several, without entering into details of the trip, claimed that their feet did not "seem to touch the ground." Emancipated from academic restraints and University authority, they had only to walk forward in the free and joyous discussion of mutual friends. With the impudence and the imprudence of youth, they said their prayers in cabarets to the sound of popping corks, jostled but obviously admired by those who served.

Francis would travel again on foot—farther and for a longer time, but without this heartwarming solidarity, without the intelligent and incisive conversation of Laynez, the sudden explosions of Bobadilla, the lofty rebuffs of Rodriguez, the gentleness of Favre.

Finally, they cast themselves into the arms of Ignatius at Venice on January 6, 1537. That curious city, supported on a forest of pilework, was still the greatest port of the world. As the center of a duchy subdivided into countless "farm states" and "maritime states," and the first Christian power to have dealt, however unsuccessfully, with the Turks, Venice was nevertheless losing its importance. This, Ignatius' group realized when they found no boat setting out for the Orient, and no such possibility for six months to come. One can imagine Francis Xavier, seeking information of possible departures on the quais of Venice, observing for the first time the great brown flanks and lofty masts of the dipping vessels, unaware that endless days of his life would be spent at sea, and in danger, before his desolate end on a small Chinese island.

Obliged to remain in Venice, they decided to offer their services to the local hospitals. Ignatius assigned the former regent of Dormans to the "Incurabili," a major establishment venerating the memory of Saint Gaetan and Saint Jerome Emilian, who had given it their particular devotion. "We had to make the beds," writes Rodriguez, "sweep the floors, clean the furniture, dig the graves, bury the dead, and be of service to the patients." This last was surely their compensation for all the rest as, in the great rooms where immense wooden trestles served as beds for several patients at once, they would hold a hand, sponge a forehead, listen to a tale of suffering . . . Up to that time, their life as students and young converts had been turned within themselves, attentive to interior directives. "I was more or less moved," writes Favre in this connection, "according to whatever element was more or less dominant within me, leading me on with more or less authority." The *Spiritual Exercises* had but increased in each one the need to advance through the thorns of his own personality not as a form of egoism, but as a conscious effort in self-experimentation. Francis was not one to follow God merely for his own salvation, but, above all, for others'. Self-knowledge alone, with an awareness of all that it requires, could lead to a real understanding of one's neighbor. In the presence of these patients, Francis must have experienced the keen interest that comes with observing how others set about facing up in a worthy manner to their tasks and suffering, as occasioned by dramas of home and profession and even by that other drama called happiness, when happiness endures beyond a fugitive moment.[12] Elsewhere the poor might perhaps have remained hidden. At the hospital they no longer kept silence; and Francis withdrew from none of them, even those smitten with "shameful" afflictions. He had not come to judge or to show preference.

In March, Ignatius called them together with instructions to leave for Rome. He himself would remain in Venice, for he feared that his presence in the Eternal City would vex two residents whose friendship he had not yet won: Ortiz, the ambassador of Charles V, and Cardinal Carafa, the future Pope, a man of violent moods and a great heart.

Once again they were on their way, and again in the rain. For three days, in their tramp towards Ravenna, they met no one. They ate green growing things and managed to ford the Po, which had overflowed its banks, by splashing through it in water up to their shoulders. While their good humor suffered no setback, they finally had enough, and artfully placed themselves on a coastal ship, which carried them into the heart of an Adriatic storm. They were without food, drink, or money, and when they declared themselves incapable of paying, the captain became justifiably irate. He put them off at Ancona, where Laynez pawned his breviary while the others begged in the streets to collect the required sum. In this they saw no cause for pity; their gaiety was winning, and money rained into their hands. With the debt settled, they treated themselves to a joyous and well-deserved meal.

After Ancona came three days in Loreto before they headed across the Apennines and the Sabine mountains towards Rome. The rain had begun once more, and they sloshed forward through the mud until at last, filthy but happy, they made their way into Rome. There the redoubtable ambassador Ortiz—whom Francis, as a son of Navarre, had some difficulty in greeting—proved kindness itself. He arranged for them to be invited to the Vatican on April third to entertain His Holiness at dinner with a theological discussion. Not in the least disconcerted, they filled the hall with their youthful assurance. Paul III, lean, elderly, and bright-eyed, was sympathetic to the enthusiasm of these young men whose keen and divers passions had once been his. It was in his blood to love human relationships, and the fervor of this little band was interesting. As an aristocrat, he appreciated Francis' fine manners, Rodriguez' elegance, Laynez' somewhat formal distinction. As Head of the Church he saw in Favre a gentle priest, sensitive and whole, pervaded by joy. A bit of mud still clung to the footgear of the Iniguistas. Paul III gave them sixty ducats to meet their needs and two hundred and sixty to finance their trip to Jerusalem. This last sum, however, was returned in short order when it became evident to them that the Mediterranean, now a theater of war, was no longer open for travel.

The comrades returned from their audience with the papal benediction and the authorization for all but one to be admitted to the priesthood. Salmeron, still too young, would be ordained a little later. In view of these prospects, the return trip to Venice, though not without moments of grave apprehension, was gayer than before, and the rain was less cold.

On June 27, 1537, for the price of a single taper, they were ordained in Venice by a Dalmatian bishop. Immediately after their ordinations, the group dispersed for forty days of prayer. Francis, accompanied by young Salmeron, took shelter in an abandoned hovel near Monselice, some thirty miles south of Padua. Each day he passed through crenelated fortifications into the little town to be given bread. On the hill above, a fortified castle reminded him of Xavier. Peaceful and clear-minded after the retreat, he rejoined his companions at Vicenza, where, in a ruined monastery open to the sky, the young men planned for the future and decided to widen their circle by visiting the Italian universities in order to draw in some intelligent youth. But for all the sun and fine air of

Vicenza, Francis and Rodriguez fell ill and were taken to the local hospice for a rest which became an extension of the Monselice meditation . . .

Once restored to health, Francis offered his first Mass in the presence of assembled friends. The weather was warm and the countryside of Vicenza was caressed by a restful sunlight. Mindful of his own extended stay at Manresa, Ignatius announced the date of departure. On the last morning, and after lengthy prayer, he told the group that they must have a name to convince authorities and outsiders of their solidarity. In their still indeterminate state, they would take the name of their Master, Jesus, as the name of their society.

Time enough later for constitutions and papal recognition. Once again, Ignatius was in no hurry.

VII

In July 1537 Francis and Bobadilla traveled towards Bologna over pavements worn white by five hundred years of light-stepping bare feet, scuffling sandals, and heavy wheels.

Ignatius' thought was that the new priests should not band together, supporting one another in a mutual strength that might mean intellectual withdrawal from the world. On the contrary, dispatched here and there in little groups of two or three, they would learn how to "establish contact," take initiative, and assume responsibility. His insistence that they remain "apart" was an invitation to personal influence. At no time did the religious association of his founding take the form of a bloc: all members of the Society were united by a singleness of vision, and unconditioned solidarity, and the idea that each, for varying reasons, had arrived intellectually at the same point. But Ignatius was firm in compelling them to scatter widely, to create spheres of influence as extended as possible without even the occasional comfort of the General's presence: to be, in effect, "apart." This confidence in his priests—a strict rule—was a form of his respect for mankind, a respect by which any true leader, whether optimistic or pessimistic by nature, has always been characterized. Not that Ignatius, the directives once given, abandoned them to their fate. His brief but occasional letters, without involving him directly in affairs to which he had not been present, gave encouraging advice. From his central position he could remain attentive while indicating the general tactical plan to be followed.

This latitude sheds light on the extraordinary instability of Francis Xavier. In India, without discipline and without constraint, as his own master—after God—he would never remain in one spot. To some, mainly to his own associates, his behavior appeared disordered; yet he would not have been Saint Francis without the strange neurasthenic crises which constantly forced him to "bestir" himself, to depart in search of another isle, another soul.[13] Arriving in Bologna, Francis found himself for the first time in full possession of this new liberty. He would put it to use and, in so doing, reveal himself.

Bologna was immediately receptive to the new priest with the heart of a Saint-Exupéry and the lean, ardent features of a Velasquez subject. Throughout his lifetime of captivating others, Francis would rarely know the spontaneous reaction elicited in the city by his fresh enthusiasm. This first mission was perhaps the most successful of all, or, at least, in a life essentially sad, the most felicitous.

The year in Bologna might be lingeringly treated in his life as a pleasant memory and the summer of his priesthood. Bobadilla had been established in the reception room of the rector of the University, and Francis was alone. For the first time he could act in accordance with his own methods and ideas, as one approved by the vicar-general of Bologna but completely independent of him. He had received only the two directives mentioned above from Ignatius: to seek out apt recruits for the Society and to essay, in the ready effervescence of this town of schools, a first maneuver against the ideas of the Reformation. Within the broad framework of these in-structions, Francis set to work. He did not seek out the students directly, but left them for Bobadilla, whose excellent argumentation could inflict well-turned, high-sounding truths on those with a preference for style.

Bologna, "the free,"[14] and "the learned," was a great city located on the Via Aemilia with a connecting tributary to the river Po, whose proximity affected the marshy site. No less important than Rome, Bologna was a beautiful city of rust-red porticos, arcades, churches, castles, and leaning towers, with extraordinary monuments such as San Stefano, built over a former temple of Isis and composed of seven separate churches—or San Petronio, begun in 1390 and already one of the world's most important shrines. Known for its religious zeal and for its fidelity to the Pope, Bologna had been attached to the Papal States in 1532, remaining nevertheless a democratic city in which the aristocracy was excluded from public office. It was there that Charles V had received the imperial crown from the hands of a terrorized Clement VII. Francis was obviously not to begin his ministry, as is sometimes the case, in a backward country town.

His first Mass bore little resemblance to that in the roofless monastery at Vicenza.[15] Within the first few days a young woman, impressed by his personality, came up to identify herself as a niece of the rector of the parish of Santa Lucia and begged him to accompany her to her uncle's house. The latter, no less impressed, invited him to remain. The young man accepted, but declined to share the rector's meals, for he had decided that as a matter of principle he would beg for his food. The expedient might be neither pleasant nor wholly reasonable, but it might serve to arouse a spirit of charity in the town.

Francis' active life was not without its reveries. His Mass might be interrupted by a period of ecstasy which lasted sometimes as long as a full hour. This tendency would surely be no drawback in India, where the tempo of life is somewhat slower. He was a friend to all, giving himself to rich and poor alike as requiring the same charity if not the same words. Neither a theologian, sociologist, pedagogue, diplomat, nor even an organizer, the future nuncio was affectionate and without sectarian spirit, peaceful in his faith if not in his way of life. As a priest, he did not agree with those who saw in the Word of God an exclusive possession of the priesthood. He neither condemned nor cut short. His seething exasperations were never of long duration; and there are many proofs that he never "preached" Christianity.

Bologna, the city of erudition, represented a normal extension of his Parisian ways. With this one exception, his active apostolate would be to the ports and harbors. Almost never, in Europe or in Asia, did he penetrate into the interior, but devoted his full attention instead to the coastal towns where civilizations meet and where he could measure the accessibility of the national fervor. Sailors and fishermen, managers and privateers, merchants and men of war were his faithful followers, and he would come to know more of the sea than any other. His restless thirst for departure might even have been called a lack of perseverance had it not been prompted by an intent to draw closer to mankind rather than to seek flight or escape. He had remained for twelve years in Paris, and this one stable moment of his life found its brief echo in Bologna.

In addition to the rector's niece, he met a woman of the streets and spoke with her in a conversation that avoided both indulgence, which would have drawn only laughter from the unfortunate creature, and categorical reprimand, painful to one already in pain. Nor did he retreat from the difficult encounter with an easy recommendation of "leading a new life" because "God is watching." For a heart so simple,

God was but an idea, God was the young priest; and to be in God's sight was to be before Francis. In going to visit her, Francis showed that he not only dared to do so, but that he was able and ready. He saw there a profound misery, the eternal symbol of that which man despoils and ruins; the stamp of ill omen sealed upon those of earth's creatures who exist without calling or belief in life, who are fated only to be plucked in unwitting harvest as a satisfaction to man's thirst instead of to his soul.

With all his activities, Francis does not seem to have gone very often to the University, which was by now well attuned to the sonorous tones of Nicolas de Bobadilla. He preferred, rather, to speak in public, teaching the children and others in need of instruction, with easy access to prisons and hospitals. An apostolate of chance and impulse, of open heart and constant watchfulness, which, with no established program, gave him the opportunity to be available to all. His poor were "the" poor; his sufferers the suffering of the world.

It was all too fine to last. Ignatius, while delighted at this development of Francis' individualism, felt that the time had come to give the Society a certain legal formality with a clear definition of each one's role. Francis and Bobadilla were recalled—not to Venice this time, but to Rome . . .

The Roman house where Ignatius finally settled was simple but expansive. It sheltered the nineteen young priests who surrounded him—and, presumably, a substantial number of ghosts. The nocturnal cracking of the great beams, however, was disregarded by the resident fathers. Francis would doubtless recall, on some Chinese or Portuguese boat, the night sounds of the house in Rome, which resembled those of a keel hard-pressed by the waves and revealing the secret vitality of inanimate objects resistant to destruction.

When he reached Rome, his eyes were bright with malaria. Nothing was then known of quinine or medicinal bark, and the disease was never to leave him. Fever produces an agitation which for some acts as a stimulant. The effect on the brain, in any case, is to reduce the invisible barrier between reality and the unreal. Francis' enthusiasms, his impatience, and his joys would always be feverish, and perhaps better so . . .[16]

Ignatius detailed him to the church of Saint-Louis, frequented by the French colony, a choice explained by the fact that Francis' French was better than his Italian. Saint-Louis was a fairly recent construction, the first stone having been laid by Giulio de Medici on September 1, 1518. Francis I had asked that the salamander, his personal emblem, be carved into the façade; statues of the kings and queens of France completed the exterior ornamentation.

For two years Francis spent the better part of his day at Saint-Louis, hearing confessions of the faithful in French and Italian. Wherever he was, confession would be of prime importance to his ministry, and his greatest gift was that of spiritual direction. Ritual, solemnity, established prayers, gestures representing secular symbols are all one-directional and lack an *exchange*. The good priest, like a good doctor, listens to his patient; both priest and doctor must know the frequent anguish of a possible error in diagnosis as they look for the imaginary in physical pain, the sincerity in a life story—fully aware that an ailment overlooked can envelop the soul . . .

Francis was not erudite. He talked, listened, smiled, and was charming, but he lacked the brilliant conversational facility which is so pleasing to the great of this world. While the subtle Laynez found his way twice a month into the papal dining room, no one thought of inviting Francis Xavier.

He who in Paris had been without nostalgia now, in Italy, felt a keen desire to go further. Having known the smell of the sea, he could not forget it, but he remained the two years in Rome. . . . It was an interesting city, washed and cooled by fourteen aqueducts and with a church or a chapel for every day of the year. From the great star-shaped pattern of ocher streets, warmed by a merciless sun, rose the basilica of Saint Peter's. Now well under construction, within seven years it was to be directed by Michelangelo. Francis strolled about the masonry as one recalling other splendid structures beginning with Sainte-Geneviève; as one loving a grandiose, monumental force bearing witness to God—a man who, twelve years later, would offer his last Mass in a little improvised chapel of brush and dried mud. A curious site, Saint Peter's—where once had been the Circus of Nero, and the enormous Constantinian church in which Charlemagne had received the imperial crown. On that site, surrounded by blocks to be adjusted and arches not yet assembled, Francis followed his own thoughts. Perhaps he was the first to pray within the vast outlines of the world's most famous basilica.

In the course of these evening walks he came to know the wretchedness of the city—all too evident behind paper window-panes, in the depths of smoky interiors, through doors left open for a passing breath of air. Such misery, essentially material and fairly normal for an era lacking in industry and household arts, might cloud the mind, as confessor-Francis well knew; but worse still could befall. The hearts of these people, after all, held a semi-awareness of God, the vague sense that a certain carpenter's Son was their Brother and Master. Both feeling and image might possibly, if not probably, acquire an eventual importance for them, especially since Europeans were more or less within the sphere of Roman influence; but far away beyond the seas were millions of lost souls completely unaware of God and, by this ignorance, not whole.

Francis constantly thought of departure, in an anguish made all the more imperious by the fact that the Moslems were overwhelming these vast countries with a viscous untruth.

The Arabian empire, professedly mystical for all its military strength, had for nine centuries been disseminating the doctrine of Mohammedanism—a doctrine which appeared to be deeply thoughtful but lacking in charity, assimilating Christianity's principles and aspirations without its historic heroism. The false doctrine produced false mentalities, while doubtless contributing a passionate note to the policy of Arab hegemony which had easily survived such local setbacks as Constantinople, Poitiers, and Granada.[17]

European powers and great colonial tracts had at that time long been virtually locked off from each other by the enormous Arabian empire of Turkey, vast as the empire of Charles V, which opened only to permit the passage of merchandise pleasing the humor and financial needs of the sultan. Cairo, with Alexandria and Constantinople as its subsidiaries, was the world's foremost market. Venice was naturally allied with the Arabs.

Since 1497, in reality, the new route, circling Africa via the Cape of Good Hope, had given the Portuguese at least a partial monopoly of Indo-European trade, to the disadvantage of Arabians and Venetians. Francis felt that the moment had come to deal the disabled infidel a blow of possible significance, to withdraw India and the Far East from Arabian intellectual influence even as they themselves were withholding their trade.

A lengthy enterprise, with the south of Spain basically Mohammedan, and France, by a terrible and dramatically mistaken calculation, no longer of the Christian union. The stratum of Moslem illusion overlying so much of the world would be difficult to penetrate, with the sumptuous taste of its architects, the passion of its poets, the attractive brilliance of outstanding artists and scholars. But this culture was one of refinement and cruelty, not of civilization.

Against heresy, *against* unbelief, *against* . . . the word supplied the Jesuits with their plan of action.

They must first of all set themselves *against* certain powers of the Church who found their particular circumstances suspect. A violent storm broke over Ignatius—not the first, but the one most dramatically destined to pelt his hopes with lively hail. "Many," he wrote, "thought that we would be burned or sent off to the galleys."[18] Yet Ignatius, faced even with the threat of annihilation, did not become unduly alarmed, remarking to one of his men that, should it happen, "a quarter-hour of prayer would suffice to restore his courage and make him resigned to the thought of seeing his work destroyed."[19] The story can be easily summarized: Mainardi, a popular preacher in Rome, was voicing ideas of Lutheran cast to which Ignatius' unsparing companions brought prompt and public attack. Spanish supporters of Mainardi rallied a few enemies of the Jesuits, among them Miguel Landivar, Francis' former valet. Too charitably forgiven for his attempted assassination of Ignatius, he had been accepted into the Society, then rejected for jealousy, fickleness, and pride. Landivar's industrious zeal quickly prepared a dossier packed with false evidence, informers' depositions, and "scandal" letters anonymous or otherwise. Much was made of Ignatius' youthful agitations, with indignant comments on Francis' visits to the "lady" of Bologna. Such muddied water produced no drama, but Ignatius, generally indifferent to gossip, was on this occasion obliged to clear Francis by appealing to the vicar-general of Bologna for a certificate. He received it, with others vitiating the enemy arguments. On November 18, 1538, the Governor of Rome completely exonerated Ignatius' friends and even praised their virtue.

The painful winter, in the words of Father Brodrick, "put a frosty crown on their rehabilitation."[19A] One tenth of the Roman population died of cold and privation. The streets filled with frozen bodies. The Jesuits took in four hundred homeless souls, and from then on, by a just reversal of circumstances, Ignatius became a "fashion" in Roman aristocratic circles. Money was placed at his disposal, and Pietro Codazzo, a secular canon of ample resources, offered both himself and his possessions.

With winter past, the Jesuits were chilled by a new drama. The Most Reverend Ghinucci, papal secretary, and Cardinal Guidiccioni, an influential member of the Sacred College, both categorically rejected the proposed constitutions of the Society of Jesus, approved hitherto in principle but without legal sanction.

Ignatius, however, had taken no risks. For three months he had spent long evenings discussing the statutes of the Order with his assembled companions. All had agreed readily enough on the principal articles, but the question of a vow of obedience had long been held in reserve. Obedience, except to the Pope, was obviously distasteful; but if the Pope were unable to attend to every detail of their affairs, they might be relegated to some unsympathetic subordinate. Nor were they inclined to select one of their own as leader. Ignatius was calling for a spirit of adherence to their controlling ideal, of detachment from mutual criticism, a spirit of equality so absolute that to endow any one with authority was already a contradiction. He himself, moreover, who would be their only choice, firmly refused to consider such an eventuality.

At long last, fearing the checkrein of directorship, they resigned themselves to the vow of obedience as acceptable only if the one obeyed were to be a member of their own group. The labored issue was at last resolved and, on April 19, 1539, the resolution taken—a step forward in the "dark light," a decision now basic to the vast unity of the Order.

The substance of their nocturnal meditations went into five chapters which Ignatius submitted, in August of 1539, to Father Thomas Badia, O.P., Master of the Sacred Palace. The latter handed on a report inviting papal approbation, and the document went next to Cardinal Contarini, a good friend of Ignatius. Contarini read the text aloud to the Pope on September 3, 1539. "His Holiness has been much pleased by the five chapters, and benevolently confirms and approves them," he wrote forthwith to Ignatius.

This was overly optimistic. The Most Reverend Ghinucci and Cardinal Guidiccioni, consulted once more by the Pope as a last resort, declared the constitutions inacceptable. Their objection was not to possible error or a mistake in principles, but to the multiplication of religious orders in general, which, in their thinking, overdivided the Church, wasting its energy and its lessons. Certain orders were vassals so important as to require concessions from the Holy See. The moment called for a reasonable centralization of Church energies, not a new group of priests.

The opposing attitudes could not be reconciled, and the Pope, despite his approval of the Society, did not wish to force his hostile counsellors. They waited a year, during which each member offered three hundred Masses, to a total of three thousand, entreating Divine Grace to overcome the resistance. At the end of that time, in a more peaceful atmosphere, the Society was promulgated.

While waiting, however, they were not unduly in need of

pity. The Pope had given them to understand that their efforts were to be directed as though the Society were officially in existence. Actually, he needed these exceptional men and was delighted to know them close at hand, responsive to his slightest bidding, and accessible without recourse to the ponderous levers of Church machinery. He made ready use of them: pontifical briefs dispatched Rodriguez to Sienna, Favre and Laynez to Padua, Bobadilla to Calabria. Codure and Salmeron, two further Iniguistas of this early group, were sent alone to carry Jesuit vigor as far as Ireland.

When it became evident that papal protection would see them to the confirmation of their Order, the Jesuits became a "must." Not a prince or duke but wanted "his." Ignatius held out against all but King John III of Portugal, whom he could not and would not resist, and whose proposals would lead to a most extraordinary grace: the sanctity of Francis Xavier. A total grace: all authentic saints are not particularly likeable, but Francis would be a most winning character as well as a hero of the Faith.

John III was a good Catholic, much concerned during his long reign with the spiritual and temporal well-being of the peoples newly subject to him. He was on excellent terms with the Holy See, despite an impassioned and overharsh treatment of Portuguese Jews and humanists which the "Renaissance" Pope—artistic, intellectual, and relatively liberal—had not the heart to approve.

Portugal was the hub of a vast enterprise in civilization and modernization: the conquest of the East by the West. This tiny country, as long as it was able, supplied motor force for the undertaking, but it was soon obliged to appeal to other nations while assimilating the foreign elements insofar as possible and insisting that their sea travel be by Portuguese ship.

The King had subsidized the College of Sainte-Barbe in Paris and was thoroughly familiar with the character of Francis Xavier, who had lived there for twelve years. Informed by Diogo de Gouvea of Francis' new turn of mind, John established contact with four of Sainte-Barbe's former students: Ignatius, Favre, Rodriguez, and Xavier.

The King's first effort at contact was not completely successful, for he did not realize that the Society was in the process of formation, with Ignatius in any case compelled to remain in Rome and the others at the service of the Pope, to whom Ignatius referred Diogo de Gouvea, John's emissary. The King immediately directed his ambassador in Rome, Pedro Mascarenhas, to request the Holy Father's approval. The Pope was delighted, but, in view of the perils of the voyage to India, he wished Ignatius to weigh the issue himself, choosing no more than two members of the Society— who, he specified, should be volunteers for this extraordinary mission. The Society numbered twenty at the time, and at Ignatius' first words, all became volunteers. For the first time he was obliged to exercise authority by making the choice himself. The decision could not be taken with serenity. Leaving for India meant leaving forever. There, where the task was done, the body would remain. After years in perfect community of spirit, there must be a farewell.

Ignatius decided on two proud and violent natures, two excellent and compelling speakers, zealous for good: Rodriguez and Bobadilla were approved by the Ambassador. A young priest, Paul, would also be assigned to them.[20] At that time —they had entered upon the interminable year of 1540— Francis was secretary to Ignatius. Furious that he had not been chosen to go to India, he performed his duties in a most perfunctory manner. "If his hands are stiff from the cold, fire possesses the property of reheating that which is ice and

can render him once more capable of picking up a pen"—
so read an amiable letter to Ignatius from a mission Father
waiting for mail.

Recalled from Naples for the great voyage, Bobadilla arrived seriously ill. Rodriguez, himself far from well, could
not wait for him and on March 5 departed with Paul. They
were sumptuously outfitted in the Ambassador's ship, since
Pedro Mascarenhas had preferred to return to Lisbon by
traveling across France.

The Ambassador's departure was set for March 15. Since
Bobadilla had not recovered, Ignatius was obliged to replace him, and his choice came painfully around to Francis,
whom he particularly loved.[21] Not that Francis was the most
articulate or the most intelligent—after Loyola, Laynez was
undoubtedly the strongest of these first Jesuits—but Ignatius
was more than touched by the young aristocrat's fidelity, by
his gracious refinement and his gentle will which occasionally
burst through its own discreet reserve to a magnificent trans-
port of enthusiasm. And Francis, one day to term himself
an "exile," would feel more keenly separated from Ignatius
than from Spain or his native Xavier.

Ignatius, nevertheless, bore without flinching the sorrow of
sending his preferred son off to India. He told him soberly
of the decision. "The Father of holy memory," he writes,
"made haste to answer: 'Forward! I am ready!' He then withdrew to make a packet of two pairs of breeches and an in-
describable cassock."[22] The deed was done. Francis was to
become Saint Francis.

Before leaving Rome, Francis Xavier sealed three letters to
be opened when the Order was definitely established. The
first gave his approval to the constitutions as they stood, and
to any additions the Fathers might subsequently make. The

second represented Francis' vote for a general of the Order, naming Loyola—or, in case of default, Favre. The third gave Laynez the right to pronounce, in Francis' name and in the presence of the new general, the vows of poverty, chastity, and obedience prescribed by the statutes.[23]

March 15 arrived. Francis left on horseback with the Ambassador and part of his entourage. Towards the end of the month he reached Bologna, where his former flock filled the church of Our Lady of Loreto as he served Mass. Out of friendly consideration, he reassumed his ministry for several days and heard the confessions of his faithful of the past. Even his companion the Ambassador came on Palm Sunday to kneel before him, thus indicating an admiration more than confusing to the young priest.[24]

Francis also paid a visit to Cardinal Ferreri, the legate in Bologna, asking him to bear in mind Ignatius' enterprises.

In Bologna, he wrote to Ignatius a letter whose beginning is not without pathos on the part of a young man of thirty-four: "From now on in this life I think we shall meet only by letter . . ." A message was enclosed for one of his Roman penitents, Faustina Ancolina, a powerful lady of illustrious birth who had poured out on Francis, and consequently on the Society, her love for an assassinated son, Vincent.[25]

From Bologna the travelers went on to Modena, Reggio, and Parma. There Francis had hoped to meet up with Favre, but the latter, unaware of their arrival, had just left for Brescia. The Ambassador dissuaded Francis from abrupt pursuit, to his keen disappointment, for Favre was his closest friend. "If we are not to see one another again," wrote Favre philosophically, "may we share together the joy of all eternity."

The journey continued pleasantly enough in spite of one incident at the Italian frontier, where they were forced to halt before a torrent so swollen with rain that all thought of crossing was impossible. One of the Ambassador's squires leaped in and narrowly escaped drowning, after which he made a deep impression on both Francis and the Ambassador "by discussing the pains of hell in a fearsome manner, as though he himself had experienced them."

The travelers continued across France and reached Fuenterrabía. The Ambassador was in haste and Francis was on the most frosty terms with relatives for whom he felt no family attachment. This may explain why he stopped at Loyola but made no detour to visit Xavier.

VIII

Lisbon in June of 1540, was an opulent capital, comparable, in all due proportion, to the London of prior to 1939: a center for trade and commerce between Orient and Occident. Hindus, Africans, and Singhalese princes could encounter one another in its precipitous streets. King John, influenced perhaps by the boldness of his navigators, had been inspired to abandon Africa for the Orient. This courageous reversal of colonial policy was served by an extraordinary man of royal lineage, Affonso d'Albuquerque, who succeeded in wresting from the Moslems several of their major settlements: Goa in 1510 and Malacca in 1511. These events were to transform European existence by supplying a practical way to fill certain needs and affording certain European sons more interesting fields of conquest than the eternal local wars in Flanders and Italy.

When Francis reached Lisbon, the achievement of the long-deceased Albuquerque was meeting with great success. John III, married to Catherine of Austria, sister of Charles V, was a contented king—and an unhappy man. Seven little princes, whom he longed to cherish, had been lost, leaving only a son and daughter, who were both introduced to Francis four days after his arrival.[26]

Dismounting from his horse, Francis was greeted warmly by Rodriguez. The latter, seriously ill, had found a tem-

porary cure in the joy of their meeting, but his fever soon
returned. In this illness, Rodriguez because of his noble birth,
was being treated by the King's doctor. He had been particularly well received in the "distinguished" areas of the city
and even exerted considerable influence over one of the
most illustrious dukes in the kingdom. He had doubtless convinced John III that the Society of Jesus was something of an
equestrian order. Certainly Father Master Francis de Xavier,
son of a once powerful minister of finance in Navarre, was
received with a certain solemnity by the King and Queen.
The first audience granted him lasted an hour. Francis, accompanied by Rodriguez, gave the sovereigns an account of
the Society, summarized its statutes, and elaborated on the
recent difficulties involved in its promulgation. The King was
most favorably impressed and pleased by the high-spirited
reserve of the young priest. Once again, charm was effective.
Francis and Rodriguez were immediately named confessors
to the pages, with rights of general supervision—a function
which, however bizarre, regularized their situation at the
court. They were lodged and fed in the palace, although they
accepted this with some hesitation, for they feared being
limited or "cut off" from the people. But it was for a short
time only, and the solution, in view of their many necessary
preparations, seemed fairly convenient. Lisbon might be the
"gateway to the Orient," but a missionary could not linger
outside the gate. Designated to accomplish in India the de-
signs of the Society of Jesus, Francis saw Lisbon purely as a
port of embarkation.

The more he pushed for departure, the more Rodriguez
tended to delay, hoping to attract one more "duke of dukes."
Excellent Rodriguez—Francis loved him deeply, but in the
end, left him in Lisbon. For the King, in his enthusiasm for
the two priests, had requested that at least one of the two

remain there to establish a house of the Order as well as a college. Moreover, the chief Inquisitor himself had dismissed a learned rabbi in order that Rodriguez might undertake his conversion.[27] Francis meanwhile tried to put himself in touch with anyone returning from Asia, and thus became the friend of the Governor, Affonso de Sousa, a veritable pirate. Friendships were Francis' weakness. To him, all geese were swans, and disillusionment filled him with sorrow. But Sousa at heart was a man of honor. For the moment, he described an enchanted Orient peopled by children . . .

For the coming mission Francis had taken on young Paul de Camérino and a former Parisian student, Mansilhas—a blunt but excellent youth not yet a priest and who, without the understanding of his master, might never have become one. Francis also accepted the services and good will of Fernandez, quite young, and a kinsman of Rodriguez. He would prove himself a loyal follower.

It was understood that John III would retain Rodriguez, yet unexpectedly he asked for Francis as well. Did he consider his own kingdom more important than Ceylon or Ternate? Nervously exhausted, spent by the heat and the uneven Lisbon streets, Francis waited. He served, it must be admitted, the Inquisition, and accompanied the condemned to the stake without interceding. A faulty idea of God was, in his eyes, the worst of misfortunes, and, if voluntary, the worst of crimes. His intelligence did not discuss the fact; the Church was necessarily right. John III had inherited from his father, Manuel I, a restless kingdom. Manuel, married to the daughter of Ferdinand and Isabella, had decreed, out of love for his charming wife, that all Jewish children were to be baptized. This meant that a considerable proportion of the Portuguese population were Catholics before the law but not by rite or desire. Extraordinary acts of disobedience resulted and were

punished by the Inquisition with atrocious, if seemingly necessary, severity. Francis subscribed to the violence of the Inquisition: he was a friend of souls but not a philanthropist.

Meanwhile, on September 27, 1540, the bull promulgat-
ing the Society of Jesus was signed. While Francis could not
congratulate Ignatius in person, it is to be hoped that he
toasted the occasion, touching glasses with Rodriguez in some
café of the "gateway to the Orient."[28] The two aristocrats
had become Fathers to one of the most aristocratic spiritual
families produced by western civilization.

After ten months of impatience, Affonso de Sousa's preparations seemed complete. At the last moment Francis'
professor-cousin, Martin de Azpicuelta, despite his forty-eight
years, had asked to leave his post at Coïmbra to become part
of the expedition. While this was no small tribute, and as
such embarrassing to Francis, the great scholar could have
brought no help to the peoples of India; both the King and
Francis recommended that he stay where he was.

For the journey the four members of the mission were
given three woolen garments as well as a quantity of books
from John III. Francis was vainly urged to take a valet at
the expense of the Crown. For books he carried only a breviary,[29] a catechism, and an anthology of quotations from
Saint Gregory, Saint Jerome, and other ecclesiastical writers.

A port is made for departures and for the sea. Henceforth,
all of Francis' missionary life would be spent in one port or
another—in fishing ports and commercial ports from Africa
eastward to the Far East. He would know them by the hun-
dreds, always burningly eager to leave once more, to move
further on, to know mixed populations and refuse no adventure. Many ships' captains, in the last analysis, have known

less of the water than he. Francis Xavier, mountain-bred, was a man of the seas . . .

Navigation was dangerous at that time, and a vessel disappeared as a matter of course before its fourth voyage. A crossing was considered perfectly safe or weather particularly clement when two thirds of the passengers survived. Waves continually swept someone from the deck; the sun produced madness; and epidemics were so much to be feared that the afflicted were cast overboard. A sixteenth-century Jesuit, Father Valignano, tells in his memoirs of the vicissitudes of such travel: "Our only food was salt fish. The passengers' throats were covered with ulcers from the salt, so they could no longer eat." As for the water, "the passengers cannot tolerate its pollution and are obliged to put a cloth before their mouths." The good Father adds: "Sometimes the majority of the passengers die—two hundred, three hundred, or four hundred on a single ship."

Francis was not hardened by his knowledge of these dramatic crossings. The Governor's fleet, delayed in the harbor by two weeks of poor weather, consisted of five ships. Francis went aboard the leading carrack, the *Santiago*.

Moreover, it was not as Father Xavier that he mounted the gangplank, but as the new apostolic nuncio to India. The Pope's parchment missive had just been put into his hands. This eminent position, the first to make a Jesuit so prominent within the Church, bears certain witness to the recognition granted this young priest "converted," if the term may be used, but eight years before, and even now only four years ordained. Francis, however, had not been among the Jesuits whom Paul III wished to have present at his repasts. The nomination, far from recognizing an intelligence impressive to the Pope, had no other motive than to give Francis full authority over the clergy of Goa, who, left to themselves, had become somewhat lax under the oriental heat. Francis, moreover, would later make only the most discreet use of his powers, seldom presenting himself as the papal nuncio. First and foremost a Jesuit, he concealed the unaccustomed honor so effectively that his title of papal representative would be quickly forgotten to the point where he would be unable to break through specific resistance by invoking an authority which his excessive discretion had essentially deprived of effect. He put the parchment in his pocket—and left it there.

Leaving the port of Lisbon was unlike leaving Paris or Rome or Bologna. Seven hundred people boarded the *Santiago* with Francis and the Governor's staff. Officers, colonial administrators, and rich merchants were cramped, with no chance to move about, into tiny overheated cabins. Women were strictly forbidden.[30] One of the four decks was reserved for a detachment of soldiers, another for the black slaves. Lastly, criminals destined for penal servitude in Ormuz or Mozambique were lashed to the rigging.

The ship sailed on April 17, 1541, his birthday, and Francis was immediately overcome by seasickness. The wind subsided only two months later off the coast of Guinea, where for forty days the *Santiago* idled under limp sails in a white calm of sun-shot reverberations. The five idle carracks, seabound in this strange absence of motion, held the men captive to their terrible calm. The four-masters were constructed entirely of wood, badly joined at the seams, so that hulls creaked ominously under great square sails of gray or brown. The superstructures fore and aft, each elevated by the curve of the hull, resembled splendidly detailed opera boxes, and the entire vessel suggested an open hand, deeply hollowed to the palm, under a cascading mass of sails, sheets, and oriflammes. These were the best ships in the world, beautiful and easily handled, but so frail that the ocean depths are carpeted with their mournful, magnificent hulks.

With the rising of the wind, the *Santiago* continued its long traditional circumnavigation of the African continent. For all the inconveniences, Francis must surely have been moved by certain new colors, flashes of brilliance, nights of velvet softness. He was sturdy enough to resist any mirage or vision conjured up by a fevered imagination; but to see all in a new way was nevertheless disconcerting to the mind and to the eye. The word "light" took on a completely new meaning in electric storms that involved all the forces of nature, almost unbearably, in a single, fantastic paroxysm. The deeply credulous may see faces in the reflection of the waves, hear voices from the sounding ship, feel a caress from the hot breath of the wind, or find the sun's rays forming brief, incandescent letters of a mysterious alphabet to be deciphered at all costs. Such are the effects of fear and fever and phenomena more than wonderful. God has so shaped the world that man can lose himself in admiration or temptation; in joy, for better or for worse . . .

Francis remained calm. He looked after the already numerous sick, and encouraged the dying. A dying man does not listen to speeches—ten words will do; and to summon up these words from the depths of heart and intelligence was the calling of Francis Xavier.

The five carracks slipped forward from one ocean to another, as the five fingers of a hand. The *Santiago*, forefinger of the hand of God, was in the lead.

IX

"Land!"

The thoughts and feelings of a *Santiago* passenger sighting the pontoons of Mozambique cannot be conceived. A boat rounding the African coastline today puts in to numerous ports en route, but the Governor's carracks had made no stops between Lisbon and Mozambique—a long resistance of men and structure to the rigors of sun and sea. Francis left the boat at Mozambique after more than four months under sail. His last dry land had been Portugal. The city occupied a narrow fortified coral island just off the coast. More appealing woodlands lay towards the interior, where Francis had no time to go. He helped to remove the sick from the boat and settled down in a cell at the hospital; then, falling ill himself, he was compelled by the ship's doctor, Cosmas Saraiva, to come on board once more and be treated in Saraiva's own cabin. It was obviously impossible to escape the *Santiago*, and Francis, never one to complain, would refer seldom, but then only with horror, to this noxious and lamentable vestige of a brilliant West. That this first lap of the trip had produced but forty-one deaths was considered the miraculous result of his holy presence; this might, also, have been just as reasonably attributed to his personal courage and kindness.

They stayed in Mozambique six months waiting for the monsoon winds. The delay might have been further extended

without Affonso de Sousa's sudden determination to appre-
hend Estevam da Gama, his predecessor at Goa, in financial
"sleight-of-hand." This darkly suggestive story was the invention of one Suarez de Mello, a captain condemned to death in
Goa, who had escaped and was seeking revenge on his judge.
He reached Mozambique with two small boats and promised
an on-the-spot revelation of Estevam's dishonesties in return
for the good graces of the new governor. Sousa, delighted to
deal this blow to a colleague and to arrive in Goa as its source
of purification—an excellent beginning for a governor—resolved to leave immediately without waiting for the April
monsoon. Estevam's brother, Alvaro da Gama, then stopping
in Mozambique, was arrested as a precautionary measure and
thrust into the hold of the *Coulam*, one of De Mello's small
boats. Sousa then took Francis on board and had them weigh
anchor immediately, leaving behind the *Santiago*,[31] soldiers,
merchants, general staff, and the four other carracks. Francis
had barely time to entrust his sick to Paul, Mansilhas, and
Fernandez.

Sousa, a pirate at heart, was highly pleased by the thought
that he might lay hold of Estevam da Gama's secret funds,
planning no doubt to appropriate them while crying scandal.
Francis, as a priest, did not become involved. Politics and
temporal quarrels held little interest for him, and his naive
friendship for Sousa remained unclouded. The Governor,
while concealing excessive greed, ambition, and scorn of
others, could evince a certain virile strength and kindliness
that left Francis conveniently free to act as an independent
within his own sphere.

Alvaro da Gama, crouching in chains in the hold where
the sound of the waves was most deafening, considered this
relationship a complicity. The fact that Francis paid him no
visit was decidedly awkward, but the priest feared to meddle

in an affair of state and, by an imprudent charity, to lose
the Governor's protection, which was so essential to any im-
plantation of the Society of Jesus in India. Francis' life carries many examples of this passionate kindness for some with
total indifference to others—proving only, shocking as it
might seem, that in the specific task which he had assumed,
no action must be disordered through pity; and proving, too,
that as a leader in the Society he felt responsible to be alert
for good days as well as poor—an administrative virtue if not
essentially a priestly one.

A strange little vessel, this *Coulam*, hugging the shore to
avoid head winds as it made its secret escape with its passengers: a governor guided by a criminal, a nuncio taken on for
last-minute good luck, and a completely innocent prisoner
whose family name was known the world over. They dropped
anchor at the Moslem port of Malindi to put off the body
of a sailor who had died during the trip; and there Francis
admired the stone cross dominating the little infidel capital.[32]
Learned Moors told him that only three of the seventeen
mosques in Malindi were actually in use; and for their benefit
he gave a description, doubtless in flourishing terms, of the
state of Christian churches. These Mohammedans who were
thus losing ground appeared more than friendly to Francis; he
was to become acquainted with Mohammedans less open to
his proselytizing.

The next stop, at the island of Socotra, where the *Coulam*
took on a supply of drinking water, impressed him deeply.
This island of aloes and incense, a valvula of the great trad-
ing zone designated today as the Gulf of Aden, had from
earliest times been a strategic spot for navigation—surveying,
limiting, even closing off all traffic between the Orient and
the Red Sea. It included two communities: an Arab majority
and a subjugated group of Christians, founded in all prob-

ability by Saint Thomas the Apostle but subsequently cut off from the Church. In the customs of these faithful there remained only the most remote traces of the Christian tradition—a moving recall of the early days of Christianity.

At Socotra, Francis was truly the successor of Saint Thomas. While assembling and re-educating the community, he reinstituted baptism and brought the faithful once again to an understanding of prayers which they had been chanting by rote in Chaldean. There was no difficulty. He was deeply respected and would gladly have prolonged the moment of joy had not the Governor, burning for the coffers of Estevam da Gama, grumblingly thrust him on board. Eight years later Francis would still have the island of Socotra in his thoughts, suggesting that two Jesuit Fathers and two lay assistants be dispatched there against powerful Turks who were carrying off Christian children for instruction in the Koran. But twenty thousand men would have been needed to liberate the island and favor the missionary cause. King John paid no attention, and little by little Christianity was totally eclipsed in the island that had known the footfalls of two saints.

On May 6, 1542, after thirteen months at sea, Francis reached Goa. There, caught under the great vault of oriental heat, the child of the Basque valleys would go forward to the needs of men without stopping to question whether he himself were happy or unhappy, well or badly off. He would show them that he was of a race who live with aim and purpose.

X

Francis' fervent faith was solid as white marble. The philosophy student in Renaissance Paris, the liberal Paris of Francis I, had discerned that behind the pleasure of open discussion lay the risk of a divided Christianity. His mind once made up, he had adhered to the Catholic Church in total submission, without reservation or problem. This, in his case, was important: the infidel must be presented with an incontestable faith. He must be first attracted, then made to feel secure.

This deliberated absence of inner unrest after the natural fevers of adolescence gave Francis, from the age of twenty-eight, considerable moral strength—perhaps even too much. He would be completely ready to enter with all possible delicacy into the mind of a Moslem or Buddhist, but the interlocutor must then wind up on his knees before the God of Christianity. Otherwise, Francis became annoyed, withdrew completely, and wasted no further time on one whose friendship did not extend to "belief." To be non-Christian for lack of instruction was admissible; but to resist was to be a potential criminal, "asocial" and "maladjusted" in the worst sense, a type of animal without intelligence or faculty of thought. On this point Francis was unwavering and intolerant—an attitude for which he has been criticized. In Portugal, he had served the Inquisition. In India, God's quarry alone would interest him. Such wings as flew away might, as far as he was concerned, keep on flying—towards the vultures.

This explains why Francis did not particularly concern himself with any study of the faiths to which he had been sent. He simply brought his own. His dislike of Moham-medanism was normal—anyone might recall how it had eaten to the core of European civilization—but Buddhism? Confucianism? Without searching the philosophy of such a belief for its own greatness or for possible points of contact with Christianity, Francis cast aside such obvious distortions of human dreaming and human respect. Neither his apostolate nor the conversions which he required to be immediate would be aided by this rejection.

Francis was too uncompromising; all saw this as the cause of every resistance to his mission. Ignatius would have recalled him to Europe, if the saint's death had not preceded the final decision. Yet a milder man, more concessive and more atten-tive to the viewpoint of others, might hardly have been a Saint Francis Xavier. Present-day accounts of how the old missionaries bring Christianity "down to native level" and include principles derived from local beliefs in order to "put it over," inspire the credulous with an uneasy fear. If the faith of Christ were to admit penetration, allowing spiritual errors in order to win the world, those very errors would little by little bring about its destruction—the inexcusable destruction of luminous truth brought by Christ's providential presence among us.

Francis need not have been excessively indulgent to native misapprehensions, but he should have been familiar with the doctrine of the opponent in order to combat and clear it of harmful elements. His numerous contacts with doctors of oriental religions, however, remained superficial. Ignatius and

Laynez would not have acted thus, yet neither they nor Francis sensed the extraordinary appeal and philosophical richness of an oriental religion such as Confucianism. Lastly, his detachment kept him from appreciating the anguish that can accompany conversion, when the conversion severs family ties, reverses an established social order, and complicates a marriage or the education of children. A conversion uprooted one's whole being; it was not the pure joy of his promises.

Francis' resistance to all native religions arose perhaps from his basic animosity to Mohammedanism, the most important of all, which already numbered thousands of Sunnite and Shiite followers and had splintered into seventy-two many-faceted sects. This belief, then as now, had a formidable tendency to fanaticize, rousing souls to a point of white heat beyond which there is no cure. The Arab world thus achieved a supranational union surpassing all treaties and left its beliefs behind to cling like a pervading glue in regions to which its hegemony has been extended. Surrounded and at a disadvantage in these areas, Christianity could gain only an occasional foothold. The high Arab birth rate, in contrast to the stable population of Christian countries, sowed widespread error over a truth whose champions were lacking in both numbers and enthusiasm.

Arrested at Poitiers in 732, Mohammedanism in 1963 extended over part of Paris. Mortally feared since the fifteenth century by all successive European sovereigns and chiefs of state, Mohammedanism sumptuously and patiently founded its empires, without disillusionment and without defeat. Xavier's disquietude is the concern of France today . . .

That Mohammedanism has been able to wear the mask of Brahmanism, even in relatively limited conditions, is an indication of its actively harmful nature. Brahmanism, serving "That which cannot be thought by the mind," is also a fairly severe social system. Its institution of castes, contrary to our notion of charity, has from generation to generation permitted the consolidation of an elite distinguished by lofty wisdom, refinement of thought, and gentleness of manner; an elite imposed on the masses and advanced by them like a rolling chariot from one century to the next. Since the Hindu god is seen as creator and final destroyer of the cosmos, a philosophy such as Buddhism might be easily assimilated under the Brahman wing. Hence, there arose no struggle for influential supremacy between these two beliefs. Buddhism was but a systematic application of the laws of Hinduism.

The Hindu places no limit on forms assumed by God, or on His incarnations," writes Usha Chatterji. "He is of all ages the Immortal, the Infinite. Various divine reincarnations and exterior manifestations have given rise to new images—not as separate divinities but as effigies of one God under varying appearances and manifestations.[33]

This god has three principal appearances, called the Triad: Brahma the Creator; Vishnu the Protector; Siva the Destroyer —differing appearances which are but particular modes of being and do not keep him from remaining the supreme being. Hindu existence seeks complete absorption in the Divine Essence, which alone brings Knowing; it aspires to complete emancipation from the illusions of the phenomenal world. This idealism had nothing in common with the brutally possessive spirituality of the Moslems—a faith based on hatred of the "false brother" and motivated by ambition for the suppression and political domination of neighboring countries; on the one hand, a temporal power artificially decked out in religious pretexts; on the other, delicate evidence of a melancholy search for eternal peace.

Francis unfortunately made no distinction between the two. He overlooked the fact that, thousands of years before Our Lord dealt with the wrath of the Old Testament, India, in its own way, had discovered the sense and superiority of goodness. There are possible points of contact between Hinduism and Christianity: the older religion—vague, appealing, penetrated with the hope of divine knowledge—might be attracted in Christianity to the specific and the precise. But Francis did not wish this, and in the long run, no one may call him right or wrong.

Goa. In their thirty-two years of residence, the Portuguese had built a cathedral, churches, and some fifty convents. "It is a sight to see," wrote Xavier, impressed, to Ignatius. The city was built on an island between two rivers, with the docks, warehouses, and shops of Arab merchants and workers taking up nine tenths of the circumference. Little by little, Portugal was to assert itself; and as the Moslems had once banished the Hindus, Christianity would banish the Moslems "by a combination of superlative courage, magnificent seamanship, colossal bluff, and basest treachery."[34] In Francis' time, however, the Portuguese minority, while Christian in attitude out of opposition to the Moslems, was basically irreligious and somewhat Hindu in cast through intermarriage. They kept as far as possible from the walls and cannon of the barbarous outskirts.

Francis took as his first residence the hospital constructed by Albuquerque—a beautiful modern edifice already "colonial" in design. He again devoted himself to his good friends, the sailors, whose needs and habits he particularly understood. The priest who had ignored Alvaro da Gama in the ship's hold now made the rounds from one prison to another, hearing confessions in rooms packed with "galley slaves and convicts, two or three hundred at a time."[35] He returned frequently to offer them consolation, scrupulously avoiding, as always, any possible confusion of the problems of charity with those of royal justice.

Not far from the hospital was the little church of Nossa Senhora do Rozario, which had also been constructed by Albuquerque. There Francis began his apostolate, giving religious instruction to a crowd of children, women, and old people whom he summoned, as he had in Bologna, by sounding a bell up and down the populous streets. To facilitate his teaching, he had set it to music that could be sung by his community inside the church as well as without. This gay and poetic approach met with instantaneous success. Rhythms scanned by a crowd, as any pilgrim from Lourdes will attest, are easily contagious.

Francis had been received on his arrival by the Bishop of Goa, a kind old man who was exhausted from administering the hottest and most extensive diocese in Christendom. Explaining his status as nuncio and emissary for the Society of Jesus, Francis placed himself entirely within the paternal hands of the aged prelate, who blessed him, wished him well, and authorized him to use his powers as he would. Once again, as at Bologna and Lisbon, Francis had no limitation on word or action.

He was naturally interested in the lepers, for whom he offered Mass every Sunday outside the town—a trip that was restful to him since he never liked Goa itself. André Bellessort gives a description that is perhaps unjust, and in any case severe for this city where life was lacking in severity:

There were numerous markets, and the morning crowds went especially to purchase slaves. Girls from all parts of India were put up . . . most of them could sew, embroider, make jam, and

play a musical instrument. At sunset another market in another
place sold weapons, old clothes, and objects acquired by theft.
At every crossroads native women would be roasting fish. The odors
of cooking and the stale smell of green leeks given off by overheated
stevedores blended in the air with the aroma of spices and the per-
fume of sandalwood . . .

Later, referring to the existence of wealthy Portuguese, he
continues:

Within this luxury and despite this nobility, greed and sensual
satisfactions were rampant. In any union of races, the individual
drawing from new customs about him is impelled to take only
those most favorable to the development of his worst instincts. The
Portuguese did not always imitate the exterior decency of the
Hindus and Moslems but borrowed from them the extreme behavior of polygamous and jealous tyrants. Weird stories were whis-
pered into waiting ears. Any death was natural, even when a
throat bore the prints of pressing fingers. The women, halfbreeds
especially, dipped unendingly into India's rich medicinal reserves,
knowing the philters for sleep, stimulation, or death. It is easy to
imagine the havoc wrought by adventurers drunken with sunshine
and impunity, in a town where the gods in their pagodas had eyes
of precious stones and the temple maidens wore rings on hands
and feet.[36]

Yet neither sun nor human lust had succeeded in extin-
guishing Christian charity in every heart. The Bishop's vicars,
Miguel Vaz and a former Franciscan, Diogo de Borba, both
priests of keen intelligence, were struck by the grace of Francis Xavier. Delighted to find at last on Indian shores a priest
equal to their needs, they turned over to him as a start the
College of Holy Faith, which was to become the first Jesuit
house in that part of the world. Sixty young men, a truly

"international house" of Hindus, Ethiopians, Singhalese, Malagasies, Malayans, and even Kafirs attended courses in the college.

Although one might think that Francis would have remained nearby, he left Goa after a mere five months; and so began—if the term is applicable to one already a year and a half en route—the life of constant shifting about to which he was apparently destined and which would find him unhesitatingly changing locations numerous enough to disconcert even a professional navigator.

A firm friendship continued to exist between Francis and the Governor, although the priest, witnessing Sousa's brusque arrival, had been present as well to his discomfiture: they had found Estevam da Gama quite ready to hand over his office, with accounts in order and the treasure well preserved . . . All must have enjoyed the joke save De Mello, the captain who had told the lie, and Alvaro da Gama, who would not quickly forget his two months in the depths of the hold.

The Governor summoned Francis with instructions to take over religious direction of the recently converted Paravas, the pearlfishers of Cape Comorin, and Miguel Vaz, as vicar, encouraged the departure. Considerable distance, more than half the length of India, separates Goa from Cape Comorin. Francis might not miss the city, but Goa would miss him. The people had come to like this unconventional priest who sat down in the evening with a tableful of rogues to bet against the devil at cards or dice, or who made himself an unexpected dinner guest in houses of scandalous domestic irregularity, ingenuously determining his host to right the situation.

Francis left Goa on September 20, 1542, and on that same day he wrote Ignatius of his regret in leaving the College of Holy Faith:

The Governor gave full support to the project. The College church —the roof is just now being set in place—is very beautiful and almost twice as big as that of the Sorbonne. The revenues are sufficient to maintain about one hundred students. Within six years' time some three hundred men of all races, tongues, and nations will have passed through here.[37]

Affonso de Sousa, meanwhile, was sounding the same note in a letter to the King of Portugal.

Although he was to complete the trip thirteen times in the course of his life, Francis' first departure from Goa caused him a sadness which to some appears touched with anguish. "I am as dust and ashes," wrote this man of thirty-six, urging—as one still a prey to persistent malaria—that Ignatius send out only priests in excellent health and begging not to be left without news of his friends in Europe. Was this merely a moment of depression, or had the state of mind existed for some time before? It is evident that Francis' character was now beginning to incline towards a certain uneasy melancholy. He was nervous and less able to overcome the fits of depression which, even ten years before his death, would seem to anticipate its coming.

The steward of the fisheries on Cape Comorin was a Hindu of superior caste who had been converted to Christianity and knighted in the course of a deputation to Lisbon. He had received his present position from King John III in compensation for what he had been obliged to suffer—without complaint—upon returning to Cape Comorin, where his conversion had been unfavorably received. Hoping that those he directed might follow his example and become Christians, he had called upon Franciscan missionaries from Cochin. The Paravas, occupying some thirty coastal villages, had been successively persecuted by Hindus and Moslems and as a result were perfectly willing to be placed under Portuguese protection if it only meant assuming the faith of their steward.

Affonso de Sousa had in the preceding years routed a last Moslem attempt at landing—with a near-suicidal boldness, for his ships had not totaled one tenth of the enemy fleet. His victory left him with a feeling for the Paravas, evinced by the sending of Francis to Cape Comorin.

The Paravas, a very inferior caste, lived, to use Francis' term, "clinging fast to the water," plunging naked into its depths with a poignard between their teeth as a protection against sharks in their quest for pearls. Skilled in holding their breath for long periods of time, they suffered from frightful asthma and frequently died young. Those who had the fortune to reach old age were no longer useful and became woodcutters in the construction of fishing boats or palm-splitters seeking the sap which, when distilled, made a powerful and soothing drink.

Francis spent two years with the Paravas, arriving with parasol, sandals, clothing, and breviary in the company of his interpreters, three Hindu clerics trained at the College of Holy Faith. They apparently landed at Tuticorin, which Francis, attracted by the peaceful shadow of its great palms as well as by the simple dwellings and easy ways of its inhabitants, made the center of his apostolate on the coast. Rarely happy, he knew happiness in Tuticorin and the villages of the Paravas, far from the colonial luxury of Goa, far from the Moslems and from the world. One of his letters observes that the fishery coast, in its complete isolation, would seem to have no landowner save God alone.

The Paravas spoke Tamil—a singsong and difficult language in which meaning is determined by tonic accent, with modulations mysterious to an outsider. Francis' interpreters did not convey its subtleties or successfully transmit the vocabulary of Christianity. He made a few independent efforts to study Tamil, but soon had enough. Applying his own method, he put the articles of the *Credo* into melodic form. Soon these "spirituals" were sung by night from one village to another . . . an instruction that cast its own spell. One does not catechize by excoriating a language, and these fisherfolk with the mentality of children were not ready for catechism. What new word of interest could be brought them by a former professor of philosophy from the Latin Quarter? An apostolate—his apostolate—of smile and gesture could bring success; poor speeches are merely a complication. In France and Portugal Francis had been most appealing and useful to others by physical charm and through the light in his eyes. With the Paravas he was constantly going from one village to another, from one hut to another, sitting with the sick, exorcizing a new mother, observing a child, admiring the catch of a good fisherman, sharing a repast of fish and rice. This tall and handsome man so open to friendship was for them more kindly than priestly. He baptized all he could, and the baptized children followed him, breaking in passage any little clay statues which represented, sometimes in pornographic forms, an incarnation of Brahma. Such baptisms, however, were arbitrary. The ceremonies amused without being understood and in the eyes of the Church have not been accepted as indubitably valid. But each to his own mission . . . Francis baptized without remorse, without consequence for others. Any little pagan may be marked by a consecrated hand; the hand of a saint leaves its trace, invisible and eternal.

Braving vipers and scorpions, Francis walked over the sand. Thirty villages, thirty thousand inhabitants. Tuticorin saw him less and less. He seldom stopped, ate little, and slept briefly. As he walked, he thrust his bare feet deep into burning sand and stepped occasionally into the clear and limpid water of the ocean to meditate before the vast unalterable expanse which never wearied the eye, never deceived the imagination. One can become accustomed to a mountain but not to the impenetrable sea.

He was fond of this country, these men, this life. "Lord, grant me not such consolations," he wrote one day in an extraordinary phrase evoking a world of rejected harmonies. Annoyed by his own ignorance of the Hindu faith, he visited a holy Brahman hermit who had attended one of the most famous monasteries in India. There he remained for some time, breaking down one after the other the reticences of this silent man, who had pledged himself to silence in exchange for the wisdom of the monastery. With the exception of minor details, they found themselves in complete agreement on the existence of a God "Creator of heaven and earth," alone capable of giving grace and help to mankind. So strong was the intellectual bond that the Brahman asked for baptism, but Francis scrupulously refused, for he found this man perhaps too far advanced in the way of faith to be treated as a mere child of the coastal region. But this friendship, persisting in all its gentleness, was for Francis a consolation.

Despite the joy of these days, Francis was very much alone among his twenty thousand Christians. The three clerics had abandoned him, and Sousa was sending no one else from Goa. Several catechists had indeed been formed, but they needed the support of others, and without his interpreters, Francis felt incapable of directing the community. This overwhelmed him, for, knowing their affection, he was confident that proper assistance could extend his influence much further to the south.

Towards the end of October 1543, his letters still unanswered, Francis returned to Goa with several young Paravas whom he wished to admit to the College of Holy Faith, which was now the College of Saint Paul. The voyage was long—they spent their Christmas on board to the sound of winds and creaking timbers.

In Goa he was surprised to find that Paul de Camerino, without consulting him, had taken on the direction of Saint Paul; but he rejoiced without displeasure as he did in meeting up with the humble Mansilhas, who, despite his dullness of mind, would be ordained. "May God have mercy on those who have given him Holy Orders. He cannot read his breviary!" wrote Ignatius to Father Lancillotto.

Although Mansilhas provided quite a contrast to the holy Brahman hermit of the fishery coast, the poor man's good will moved Francis to conceive an affectionate attachment for him. Francis' own kindness and loneliness in unusual circumstances made him take Mansilhas as a confidant, familiar, and brother, on whom, in the sad comedy, he came to depend.

As soon as he reached Goa, Francis began recruiting for Cape Comorin. Only three prospects were given to him: two priests—one Spanish, one Hindu; and a Portuguese gentleman of aimless existence. As soon as the group was formed, he left without extending his visit to Sousa or to the new director of the College. Had he made the long trip only to leave so soon? Would he not have been more useful at Goa? Did he stop to reflect on his function as nuncio and his responsibility as co-founder of the Society of Jesus? Not at all: he set sail for the country of the Paravas, the country of friends . . .

The boat put in at Cochin, close to their destination, and there, seated perhaps on a coil of rope or heap of sails beneath

the shadowy masts, Francis undertook a letter to the Fathers
in Rome. Harbor sounds did not disturb him—the cries of
merchants, the grating rub of the boats, the sudden wild spray
tossed up by water lying captive between two hulls, the heavy
tread of hauling oxen. He felt far removed from the Fathers,
as one who had been long away seeing things they had not
seen: aspects of the world and of Christianity inconceivable
to the Roman imagination. He was alone and responsible for
souls resistant to any European method of approach. He wrote
on and on without stopping. The lengthy monologue, dated
January 15, 1544, became a veritable sheaf of papers, treating
all subjects with great charm of thought and style. Its eventual publication as a small volume attracted considerable attention throughout Christendom. The book gives a clear
picture of a missionary's role, for which it became in a sense
the guiding work. Francis de Xavier, leaning against some bar-
rel in the port of Cochin while the sun burned into the stuff of
his parasol, produced a work which great writers could not
have improved.

His second year in the south of India, by way of contrast,
bore no resemblance to the first, as former joy yielded painfully to bloodshed along the beautiful coastline. Trouble arose
with the installation at Tuticorin of a Portuguese captain,
Cosmas de Paiva. Francis' influence had drawn interest to
the place, and the Paravas were considered sufficiently developed to warrant official protection. Paiva, however, began
by arresting and selling a number of young Christian women.
Xavier's thunderous attack fell on a heart of stone.

Things were differently organized now that Francis had the
assistance of Mansilhas and his faithful catechumen-shadow,
Matthew. Anxious to avoid meeting the arrogant Paiva in the
streets of Tuticorin, he withdrew to establish Mansilhas in

the coastal port of Manapad, where he occasionally joined him; [sending him hither and yon and writing bi-weekly instructions as he himself traveled from one village to another.]

Mansilhas had become in a sense the administrator of the community,[38] but because of his uneven temper, he was accepted solely as Francis' representative. Sensing that trouble lay ahead, he became unusually severe. Any woman arrested for drunkenness was immediately consigned to three days in prison. As with all priests past or present, Francis was far more indulgent to the faults of a man than to those of a woman. He implied that, through Mary, God would be compassionate and gentle with men; with women, on the other hand, he would be more severe than a strict husband. His success among these toilers of the sea was nevertheless somewhat unusual in that he actually succeeded in breaking their taste for liquor.

The war, foreseen by Mansilhas, broke out at that time and was disastrous to the land of the peaceful, hardworking Paravas. Two enemy rajahs took the coast as their battlefield; Paiva, motivated by self-interest, surrendered the fishing villages to the rajahs' recurrent fury, to be taken, retaken—and finally destroyed by a third intervening force of savage Badaga warriors, a cruel and retarded race who galloped down to the sea from the north, leaving terror and desolation in their wake. The whole affair was a hornet's nest without reason or issue, which covered the south of India with a swarm of combatants unable to tell friend from enemy. In this total confusion, general massacre—a wine more heady than that of the palm—was the way of least resistance. Conflicting forces met head-on without daring to attack or support, blending finally into a shapeless amalgam of those who could ransom or crush, buy up and then betray.

Never was Francis' silhouette more in evidence than against this flaming sky. Determined to evacuate his Paravas, he passed untouched through every fiery encounter—suggesting himself as arbiter between artful Hindu princes who seemed to listen; paying off ransoms; negotiating truces; helping the most unfortunate. When communications were severed from one region to another, he chartered a small boat laden with provisions and traveled by night—avoiding treacherous reefs —to the point under heavy attack. He threw himself into the thick of every fight and organized a man-to-man food supply without receiving a single scratch.

Paiva saw his ships and houses go up in smoke. Any Parava who could, abandoned his scorched straw hut and took refuge among the boulders of the coastline, where the Nordic hordes, [having unwisely set fire to Portuguese and shipping boats instead of confiscating them,] could not pursue. Once on dry land, they stopped to regain their breath. Finally, there were treaties and agreements, and the war was over. Booty was parceled out and everyone returned home except the youngest slaves, who were put in chains. Francis could only rebuild and reassure his understandably disillusioned Christians on the question of Portuguese support. The task was not impossible, and life went on, untouched by bitterness in its tranquil, age-old rhythm. The recent combats had endowed the Paravas with only one new taste—force—with the result that the "wealthy," to be reinstated, were first deprived of their immediate possessions. Father Mansilhas, despite his surly manner, could handle the emergency while Francis made his dispirited way from Tuticorin to Manapad.

His trip included a reproachful visit to one of the misguided warrior princes, who, to remain in the good graces of Father Xavier, gave him the right to sow the Word at will throughout the lands of western Cape Comorin. For Francis, this meant that the Christian "pocket" of southern India might double its strength. He needed no second bidding, but his enthusiasm was not the same. Even in the calm moments of 1543 he had not been fond of India; now he did not like it at all.

From Manapad he went on to Cape Comorin, where various questions had to be settled with the Governor's emissary, and thence to the camp of his friendly rajah, from which he started for Cochin on foot by traversing the kingdom of Travancore, whose souls had been entrusted to him. It was hazardous to travel unprotected through provinces which were without central jurisdiction or the local patrols of minor self-styled kings, but Francis was so exhausted that he had only a vague idea of the actual dangers involved. He walked by day and prayed by night, constantly imperiled by tigers, jackals, and reptiles while myriads of fireflies filled the shadows with their emerald lamps. He might have had as an ancestor some venerable captain-explorer, equally determined in the pursuit of a fixed goal.

Rain, wind, deserts, and trackless mountains could not discourage him, though he was no longer sustained by the strong morale of the past. "I am so weary of living that it would be better to die," he writes—but for the Faith, and not as a prey to wild beasts in this country of his desperate advance.

Finally he reached Travancore.

This wretched country, a land more ungrateful than the fishery coast, was most receptive to one whose arrival had been "drummed ahead" at the rajah's orders, and within a month he knew every corner. He used all possible means to awaken a response, with the result that his month's record far surpassed that of two years with the Paravas: ten thousand men, women, and children were baptized—not out of zeal, for Francis considered the effects of an overhasty act highly suspect—but in final hope, and with reflexes of pain. He was leading an inhuman life. The soul was immortal but not the body.

The lagoons of Travancore were kind to his feet, but in this country the land rises rapidly to the loftiest mountain peaks south of the Himalayas. Francis sought souls as another might have hunted eagles' nests—and in an ecstasy of kindness drew this entire people to his arms: within a month they were morally purified and almost entirely Christianized. This flash apostolate achieved rapid acclaim and did more for the glory of Saint Francis than other more rational accomplishments. No subsequent missionary group, with all the propaganda at its command, has drawn so spontaneous a flame from the faith of a slumbering race.

It was at Cochin that he heard the first account of a tragedy which, for his already wounded heart, would make India almost unbearable.

The island of Ceylon, opposite Tuticorin, lies along the extreme southern coast of India in a shoulder formed by the Gulf of Palk. No other island has given rise to such charming legends, and Francis, the perpetual traveler, expected the trip to be easy. The island was shared by numerous kings whose luxuriant mutual hatred could be found only in such a paradise of nature. Its "great" families could tell of assassinations, rape, and betrayed promises, while the Portuguese, entrenched in their small fort of Colombo, avoided imposing order but lent their solicitude, properly directed by the clink of coins, to one side or the other. These kings were opportunists, sacrificing the souls of their subjects to the god of Portugal according to the necessities of the moment. When the urgency became less manifest, they rubbed baptismal water from their foreheads and closed the flowered frontiers to Christian influence.

The King of Jaffna, whose long ascent of the royal tree had been made with dagger in hand, now ruled over the little Singhalese island of Manar. His subjects had been told by the Parava fishermen of the changes Francis had made in their lives, and they asked him to come to them. A charitable Hindu priest, sent before, had founded a promising little community of six hundred baptized, but the King, fearing that obedience to God or Francis Xavier might preclude an obedience due first to him, would not tolerate this "state within a state." He had the priest and the neophytes, none of whom would deny the Faith, massacred in cold blood.

The oldest brother of the King of Jaffna had previously missed his moment to claim the throne. Now, seeing this provocation of Portuguese wrath as another opportunity, he traveled to Cochin, where he found Francis sunk in sorrow, despite any comfort he might derive from the thought that a land of Christian bloodshed is thereafter Christian in itself. The Prince swore to become Christian with all his subjects if Portugal would give him the throne of Jaffna. Unfortunately, however, several Christian Singhalese kings had similar aspirations for their sons and went directly to Sousa. Francis hastened to Goa, where Sousa heard him through, raised his eyes to heaven at such a recital of misfortunes, and promised to consider. Actually, Portuguese arms could not be drawn against Christian kings of Ceylon for an unbaptized prince. To dispose of the crown of Jaffna meant that it must first be won . . .

The indefatigable Francis again traveled around the Indian coast to watch the formation of an avenging armada at Negapatam, opposite Ceylon. But there was no armada. The murderous king had seized a Portuguese ship which had been in straits offshore. The ruler of Negapatam, exclusively preoccupied with recovering its rich cargo, chose to negotiate and overlooked the martyrs.

Souls are souls. Gold is gold. Sick at heart, Francis gave up the cause.

Father Xavier, so independent himself, left complete independence to those under his authority. His letters to the Jesuits of Goa seem to contain advice rather than directives, the execution of which, with apparent indifference, he never verified. Learning that two new Fathers recruited for India by Rodriguez had arrived in Goa, he never went to see them. Francis chose, for the moment, to forget the beautiful capital of falsehoods, where he had so tugged at the bit—and where mankind has since committed him to sleep forever in his tomb. A brief stop in Cochin, where he waited in January of 1545 for a boat to Negapatam, was to decide the future of his mission. There he settled himself once again amid the kegs and cases of the docks, surrounded by ropes and chains and broken buoys. The ships along the waterfront, their extended sails forming a kind of roof, had become a great continuous hucksters' market illuminated throughout the night by yellowish lamplight.

One year after his voluminous message to the Fathers in Rome, he was maintaining an extensive daily correspondence. He had decided to leave India, and all must first be in order. On this waterfront, where his cassock and parasol had become a familiar sight, he was now being drawn into new encounters and conversations.

On January 26, 1545, when he had been perched on his coil of rope for six days, writing letters to Europe and watching the departing ships, a traveler from Malacca, Antonio de Paiva, arrived, who supplied him enthusiastically with descriptions of the Molucca archipelago. The next day a Christian prince from Ceylon came, the nephew of a Singhalese king, who would await his uncle's death and then, as his successor, introduce Christianity into the little forest kingdom. Francis felt compelled to leave. Far off, a marvelous archipelago lay waiting for conversion, and nearby the Christian hearts of Ceylon seemed ready to kindle by themselves. He might entrust the smoldering flame to others and sail on to Christian countries of the future.

These insights and the overwhelming thirst for departure which possessed this most itinerant of saints are transcribed into the Cochin letters. There was one for King John III—strong, direct, and somewhat arrogant, containing a biting, man-to-man criticism of colonial administration as a luxury affair grown indolent in the heat. He supported his good friend Miguel de Vaz in an imprudent request to be named Inquisitor for India. There was also a letter for Ignatius, like that of a faithful correspondent complaining to one whose answers rarely came: "During the four years of my absence from Portugal there has been but one letter from you . . ." The simple statement reveals his loneliness. He also wrote to the Fathers in Rome, and, lastly, to Simon Rodriguez.

Amid somewhat rambling, albeit charming, discussions, Francis stresses the great basic need in India for many additional priests, no matter what their state of health. This had not been his previous contention. India, he now claimed, must be filled with Jesuits, for all past setbacks derived from a lack of ways and means.

These letters are written on a note of hopeful optimism which is far from characterizing the entire correspondence. In Europe, perhaps because of the "miraculous" Travancore conversions, they achieved greater renown than those of the preceding year; and, at the King's request, excerpts were read from every pulpit in Portugal. Favre, in Madrid, had copies sent to King Philip II.

The packet of documents having been sent, Francis sailed from Cochin. After a short and disappointing stop in the deserted port of Negapatam, he went on up the coast of Coromandel towards San-Thomé. It was March, and the half-empty little vessel on which he had taken passage was seized by a crippling tempest that lasted all through Passion Week. The ship was obliged to put back into Negapatam, where Francis resumed his writing. With the second attempt, however, came fresh storms, and this time he resolved to make his way over dry land. The trip under the May sunlight would be a test of endurance, but Francis was fascinated by the thought of seeing the tomb of Saint Thomas and of being able to pray beside his predecessor of centuries before.[39] Two hours of hot desert sun can catch the breath and fill the mouth with sand from a spiny and ungrateful golden landscape, but Francis walked forward. He had been walking for four years.

The four months at San-Thomé formed a rare and benign moment of complete retreat necessary to his physical and mental equilibrium. As the guest of the pastor, Father Coelho, he spent the time in meditation. The rectory, located just outside Madras, consisted of a small one-room house with a kitchen and a tiny garden overlooking the sea. Close by, and hidden by the trees, stood the little chapel and tomb of Saint Thomas, relatively forgotten in its obscure location but venerated at one time—according to Marco Polo—by Christians and Saracens alike. The little harbor of Mylapore, with San-Thomé as its residential section, was tranquil and luxurious. While taking every advantage of his rest, Francis would occasionally emerge from the garden to surprise amorous couples —drawing together the unwed, persuading others to give up a forbidden fruit. In a short time this fraternal, white-robed personage had effected weddings and reunited fiancés, teaching them a joy beyond mere joy of living . . . Far into the night he conversed with Father Coelho, who was overcome by the presence of so renowned yet so simple a guest. Francis talked with him of Paris and Sainte-Geneviève, and of Sainte-Geneviève's little compatriots, the "girls" of Paris. He laughed to recall the temptations of his youth which had given way in subsequent years to many others, while Father Coelho's eyes opened wide at the very thought.

In the late hours of the night Francis prayed beside the tomb—Saint Francis confronted by Saint Thomas. Certain nocturnal incidents may never be verified—but in any case, several times the pastor thought he heard Francis combating devils in a little garden shack, while Francis himself heard matins sung in the chapel choir behind locked doors where none could go.

But the apostle to the vastness of the Indies could remain no longer within a curate's garden.

XI

In September 1545, Francis embarked for Malacca. For three and a half years India would be left to itself and to the young Fathers from Rome. The attentive care of San-Thomé's placid pastor, for whom earthly well-being still held some savor, had restored his health; but his strength was immediately tested by a storm that descended on the ship, frightening crew and captain alike.[40] Lightning flashes before the plunging prow revealed liquid depths which seemed to lie in wait for a crashing ruin. Francis suffered, as he had suffered before, but he remained on deck clinging to ropes and railings, encouraging the sailors, and, sometimes days in advance announcing their arrival—perhaps through Grace, or perhaps because his previous navigation had enabled him to estimate from appearances the probable advance of the ship.

There is no recovery from Malacca. Venice, Lisbon, Goa, and Cochin are great harbors and important storage centers of intersecting streets. Malacca, its serried ships comprising more of a city than the town itself, was no different; yet it was something else besides: a place God chanced to touch in forming the earth; a city already blessed in its pagan state, though unhappy, for happiness comes from moderation and control, a reasonable harmony of elements. Malacca was caught, as a cloud between pressures, by gleaming waves and streaming rivers of sunlight—a hot city turning now red, now gold, now brown within the Asiatic oven; a noisy city where rasping instruments rhymed the hours; a city of flowers and palaces and curving hills from which watchmen might survey the sea; a paradise built of its own ocher clay to await embellishment by the enchanted Albuquerque; a fine city for Malays and Chinese; a home of merchants and poets, where secular intelligence was counterbalanced by the vibrant heartstrings of the poor . . .

A tranquil river, crossed by red bridges, coursed through the city, giving an impression of coolness, but changing a few miles upstream to a rushing torrent of gold-shot pebbles. Water buffalo descended into this river to breathe deeply, gray nostrils uncovered, in safe protection from the sun and the flies. In the artisans' quarter, where paper drawings rattled with an occasional wind, there was a separate street for each trade. Within this anthill of red ants, this spaceless, shapeless city, Albuquerque had constructed administrative edifices, a fort, and a noble church—Santa Maria del Monte. Francis would open an avenue to God.

Father Xavier reached Malacca for the first time as an honored guest. He was now well known as occasional advisor to the Governor. Nearly every captain had had him on board, and all had seen him at Cochin or elsewhere, penning voluminous letters from his perch on a coil of rope. His charity without austerity, his deliberate kindliness, the boldness of his actions and his smile at the first sight of land[41] had prepared a ready welcome wherever he was expected; and all expected him. Unceasingly, in ceaseless India, his tasks went on.

One lone priest was directing the Christian community of Malacca with difficulty, for Malay arms were stronger in embrace than those of the Hindus, and souls were sluggish from the easy life. This state of affairs was disquieting to Portuguese administrators, who entrusted to Francis the moral alignment of his fellow citizens. It was a new mission since his previous work had dealt only with natives. Now he was being asked, in the King's name, to bring God back to the conscience of supposedly civilized creatures who lay stretched out, unthinking, in the shadow of the palms.

Francis blessed the crowd that came to meet him, and, in touching the heads of the children, apparently "miraculously" called some of them by name. (It is more probable, however, that his words were sufficiently apt to convey that impression.) It was immediately obvious that Malacca was not India. The Portuguese in Malaya, despising the Hindus and detesting the Arabs, had become friendly with the Chinese, with the result that their form of colonization had become something of a cooperation between two races capable of mutual esteem. For the Chinese, such respect could as easily be extended to the Portuguese religion.

Francis stayed once again at the hospital, sounding his little bell by day in the streets. He was frequently the guest of rich Chinese merchants, but his Portuguese relations remained limited.

For all his kindness, he could upon occasion become very demanding. Such was the case with the trafficking subject of John III, Juan de Eyro, who, by ravaging the seas and shores of India for most of his life, had amassed a considerable fortune. Now an old man who had shops, women, and a fleet, he had no God but aimlessly wandered from port to port until Francis stunned him into belief. The conditions were severe: Juan must sell his fleet and merchandise, and give his money to the poor. When he had done this (withholding a modest secret reserve), Francis summoned him to San-Thomé, and for three days, in the little garden cabin, drew forth the confession of this wounded soul. Juan was left weakened but strangely happy. At the end of the confinement, the new Christian went for a walk along the waterfront. His former passion once again overcame him at the sight of a boat; and, hastening to produce his last supply of gold, he immediately negotiated for the purchase of ship, crew, and cargo. The affair concluded, he ascended, firm of tread, to the deck, thinking to put considerable distance between himself and Francis Xavier —at which point a small boy hailed him with "The Father wants you!" Juan de Eyro was a true Christian; he swore roundly—and left the ship, to follow Francis to Malacca.

There an alms-gift provided this man of no means with an occasion for sin; and an informed Francis dispatched him in penance to a neighboring island, where the poor contrite pirate became subject to visions: Jesus was calling him; he was being rejected by the Blessed Mother. He becomes rather a pathetic character, this man of wealth reduced to beggary by Francis, who from then on would lend little or no support, surrendering him to the sufficiency of Divine Grace. One can nevertheless imagine the giggling girls of the waterfront, the imposed vexations, the sailors spitting at the feet of him whom they feared . . .

As for Father Xavier, he had been unsuccessful in his attempts to penetrate into Malayan households. The Malayans were Mohammedan with no thought of change—and, moreover, they were too lazy to become involved in the difficulties of assuming a new religion. Christianity—and Francis—would lose with regret a refined people so childlike and yet profound. One may or may not be attracted to this race of magicians and spiritists with their world of unreality, but to give them up is to miss one of the great charms of the Orient. Yet because Francis was unable to convert a single one of these closed minds, he quickly lost interest. After all, he had not come to waste time dreaming with dreamers.

The Malay spirit, while tending naturally to cast out the terrors of its collective wisdom, has remained primitive; and the Malayans are extremely responsive to beauty. Their charming dwellings, the most humble almost as lovely as the most noble, are thatched with dried leaves, patiently sculptured into a veritable lacework, and can be easily taken down and moved, in case of a death, to another spot. Depending on the trees for their support, they have filled the Malay forests with tens of thousands—each a tasteful and lovely miracle of delicate workmanship, skillful arrangement, and inventive ability. Yet Francis Xavier, whose handsome charm should have won their hearts, was too positive to attract the people—and he stopped seeing them. The true nature of his reactions cannot be known, but it is difficult to believe that he did not cast at least an affectionate glance towards these fever-ridden farmers so devoted to their rice and to their demons; and it is difficult, too, to believe that he could establish no contact of any kind with one of the world's most dynamic and appealing peoples.

Pleased by his relationship with the Chinese, disappointed in the Malayans, and content with the Portuguese, who at least displayed a degree of good will, Francis was less overwhelmed by his task than he had been in India. At night he was drawn irresistibly to the waterfront, the boats, and the sailor yarns—strange tales to quicken his interest. He heard rumors that beyond the peninsula lay the Moluccas, a fantastic group of small volcanic islands topped by disordered groves of cocoa palms and intriguingly inhabited by small unguided tribes. Francis, watching the gentle roll of the ships, determined that one of the vessels would soon have him aboard.

To leave Malacca, however, was to create despair, for he was greatly loved. He had found good husbands for attractive girls; he had played cards for hours on end with a soldier who was resisting temptation; and on occasion, when dining with a bachelor, he had asked afterwards to speak to the concealed concubine, whom he would greet with respect, praise her cooking, and thereby restore dignity to the little fallen creature without offending the master of the house. With all his activity, however, Francis had never lost the habit of profound meditation; and no matter what he was doing, was able momentarily to retreat within himself.[42] His nights, which were often wakeful, were partially spent in deep thought. In Malacca his intensive discussions with a Jewish scholar whom he later converted led him to resume, though without benefit of the Paris libraries, his somewhat forgotten use of dialectics. At night he moved through the streets, singing with the children, and the laughter of cabarets would be arrested by the picturesque and enchanting sight. Children would always be ready to sing with Francis Xavier.

Leaving these friends, Francis embarked on January 1, 1546. He had spent three months at Malacca—months which figure in his life as an extension, in similar vein, of the admirable days at San-Thomé. He chose to avoid Macassar, capital of Celebes, where Christian penetration had been compromised by a minor burlesque drama. A prince of the region, converted by a priest from Malacca and subsequently gratified by John III with the renowned royal title of Don, had entertained an officer of the Portuguese navy at dinner. The latter, regaining his ship after the banquet, had taken along the daughter of the Prince as a dessert . . . This sentimental pleasantry had so discredited the cause that Francis decided to sail instead directly to the Moluccas, through islands scattered over the sea "as birds after a storm."[43]

The Moluccas were an archipelago blanketed by clove trees; and their yield, used in cooking, medicine, and perfumes, found a ready market the world over. To govern the entire group of islands, Albuquerque had sent Captain Antonio Galvao, who stayed there two years. Galvao was so honest that when he left he was in poverty, so good that he left highly respected. Because of him the Portuguese were fairly well accepted by the simple natives, to whom all strangers appeared as devils spit from the sea.

Francis landed on February 14 at Amboina after a long trip. While the shores of Sumatra, Java, and Borneo had left him unmoved, he had at last reached that part of the Far East where the climate is most agreeable and the scenery most extraordinary. He was soon at home in these islands, yet he was unable to give them his immediate attention. A fleet of Portuguese warships[44] carrying Spanish prisoners had dropped anchor at Amboina, and Francis came to their aid, encouraging and hearing confessions before he went inland, where he discovered seven isolated Christian villages.

Hoping to visit every island—there were "too many to count"—he set foot on land wherever possible, nearly always encountering the same cruel and savage headhunters, who streamed down from mountains where they were constantly at war with one another. Writing to summon Mansilhas, Francis urged that he bring with him "a chalice of copper. Out here it is more safe than silver."

Distances between the islands are relatively short, yet more than once the boat was buffeted by winds. On one terrifying occasion, Francis fastened his crucifix to a cord and suspended it in the water to calm the high seas. A wave snatched it away, leaving him inconsolable, but the next day while walking on the beach at Ceram, he saw a crab moving towards him, the crucifix held firmly between its claws . . . The tale is no invention and need not be considered a miracle. Those who have journeyed much, as Francis had, can tell equally strange stories . . .[45]

At the end of three months, with Amboina as his home port, Francis had baptized more than one thousand people and established a Christian community. He set forth for Ternate in an open, low-riding boat which was manned by oars. The crossing, accomplished to the rhythm of tom-toms, was like a leisurely walk about the islands. Ternate was nothing more than an active volcano which spouted fire from its summit. Its slopes were covered by somber forests which concealed icy torrents, and the beaches encompassing the island were slight. The people were of Malay extraction, and, despite Portuguese occupation, were pagan. Recalcitrants from Goa were deported there.

Francis liked the island and decided to win its people. In his usual compelling way, he sought out the children and established a singing group. "It has become a custom," he wrote, "for boys in the streets, women and young girls at home, or workers in the fields to sing religious songs day and night."

The cloves were harvested in August and September. Francis, inactive for this part of the year, began to compose a small book. Writing was evidently easy for him. In his numerous letters, where sentences accumulate for better or for worse, where words are correctly or incorrectly used, the writer's personal charm stands revealed—with one, ten, or fifty pages preceding the signature. This facility of expression led him to produce a modest work on the pleasant shores of Ternate, while he rested at last in the shadow of tamarisks and the wings of tropical birds. The book was devotional, unfinished, and destined for no one in particular. It is somewhat dry in comparison with his letters, taking its tone rather from the *Exercises* of Ignatius—Francis had forgotten his one-time humanism. By chapter nine, overcome with the heat, he had put down his pen. Then, once again, he rose for departure—refusing to relax into well-being and lose his own glory among the glories of nature.

The island of Morotai, or Morty, is reached by rounding the Moluccas to the north. Its coral defenses concealed a human hell which would seem to exist only to reassure the civilized of their civilization. The island belonged to the sultan of Ternate, who carefully avoided any visit to its savage inhabitants. Francis, against prudent friendly advice, landed there at the end of September.

He has hardly referred to his three months' stay save to observe that the inhabitants—understandably—could not read or write, but they knew every poison and used them. The men wore garments of bark and occasionally, out of madness or hunger, killed their women and children to devour the tender and succulent flesh. Francis became the true explorer of this forgotten spot, walking alone over the mountains and smiling when he met a savage, whom he would then hasten to embrace. An astounding apostolate—all the more astounding in that he was not killed and cut in bits a hundred times over . . . He was well aware that his procedure was dangerous and that, in God's name, he was advancing through a terrestrial Valley of the Shadow. A letter sent to the Fathers in Rome before his departure is poignantly sad: "I beg you not to forget me. I live in such need of your help. For my great comfort, and to keep you always present, I have cut from your letters the signatures, written out in your own writing, and I carry them always with me." Xavier, a collector of autographs, carrying the signature of Ignatius about with him as an invincible talisman . . . All of the above appears in print as half adventure, half exploit—between Alexander Dumas and the Grail legends, with a touch of Agatha Christie. Yet its reality conveys an idea of the life of a saint. Man is made in God's image, and our human condition is to surpass a norm.

Francis' final comment on his three months among the world's most inveterate assassins was courageous in its humor: "They were a great comfort to me, *and I to them.*"

With no great illusions as to who might have heard the Word of God, spoken thus to the winds on the isle of Morotai, he returned to Ternate and remained until Easter of 1547. From there, escorted briefly by torchlit barks—the faithful thus deferring the moment when they would no longer see the man they loved—he continued to Amboina, and from Amboina once more, through a paradise he again resisted, to Malacca.

The captains along the waterfront were no doubt delighted to have him back in one piece.

XII

In Malacca, Francis found the two Jesuit Fathers whom he had designated to carry on the mission of the Moluccas. Mansilhas had mistakenly sent a substitute; he would have enjoyed Ternate, but he was becoming crotchety, as can frequently happen to the weak and overburdened. Moreover, he was soon to leave the Society—whether he was rejected or withdrew from a sense of ineptitude has never been made clear. In any case, the future would find him with only good to say of Francis, as a grumbling but faithful valet might praise a former master, the only one who had made something of his arid personality by giving it a moment of expansion.

The two Fathers, alternately astounded and overwhelmed by Francis' accounts, were sent on without delay to lessen as much as possible the transition between his departure from the islands and their arrival.

Word of Favre's death must also have reached Francis at this time. A bond of twenty-one years that has met with no obstacle is strong, especially when it is intellectually rooted in similarity of vocation. Favre and Francis, by nature affectionate, had allowed affection to enter their friendship not as an indulgence, but as a supplementary means to good. Priestly friendships, friendships of the unattached, because they have no need to withhold a professional or family secret, can be more absolute than others.

Francis felt his loss keenly. Favre in Heaven was obviously closer and could see and be with him, but a friend in Heaven is not accessible for immediate advice, and there would be no more letters. God's Kingdom will be ours, but it is of the other world, and even so accustomed a wayfarer as Francis could not think of it as immediately adjacent. Grief and fatigue made him irritable, and the arrival of Moslem pirates in the Bay of Malacca called forth in him an unaccustomed anger.

When the Moslem attempts to land proved unsuccessful—seven Malay fishermen, losing nose, ears, and feet to the faithful disciples of Mohammed, were the only victims—the Portuguese prematurely toasted one another in self-congratulation. Francis and several young officers eager for a fray called for pursuit of the small, lateen-rigged pirate craft, and Francis, called "creator of the armada" by the Captain of Portugal, organized the outfitting of a fleet of ten vessels. Three weeks went by with no news, and enthusiasm gave way to gloom. The Captain was concerned that his area was no longer protected, for he knew that the sultan of Johore was finding the moment suitable to assemble a hasty invasion fleet while his spies spread rumors of disaster through the streets of Malacca. Francis, primarily responsible for the chase, uttered vain words of assurance and felt his reputation at stake.

On Sunday, December 4, he announced formally from the pulpit to a turbulent crowd his presentiment of Portuguese success, and repeated the message that evening in another church. Everyone took heart, and it was later learned from first arrivals that the day in question had given the Portuguese their final victory over the Moslem pirates.

Did Francis have a true presentiment, or was he confident of a victory that God must necessarily give to the Christian cause against the infidels? Did he mean, with his announce-

ment, to create new confidence that might crush the dangerous wave of anarchy and defeatism that swept over Malacca?
Or did he feel that imminent revolt justified his playing his
whole hand? A physician's sympathetic promise of improve-
ment would on occasion annoy him beyond measure. Are the
laws of human destiny inflected by the hope that passes from
one to another?

It was during this same month that Francis met for the
first time a man who, next to Ignatius, would be the most
extraordinary determining influence on his life. Once again a
strange story was involved. In 1542, the year of Xavier's arrival from Europe with Affonso de Sousa, three Portuguese
merchants en route to China were beached by storms on the
coast of Japan. Japan at that time was totally unknown, and
the men were understandably terrified. However, they were
reassured by a young man of thirty-five named Anjiro,[46] who
belonged to an illustrious family in Kagoshima, a well-known
harbor on the great island of Kyushu. Anjiro's profound rest-
lessness had forced him to drift aimlessly about although, he
told the merchants, he had spent some time in a Buddhist
monastery, where he had vainly hoped to find peace. Now he
was plunged in a despair from which neither his wife nor
children could distract him, and the merchants, although they
sympathized, could do nothing for him.

Two years later another Portuguese merchant, Alvaro Vaz,
entered Kagoshima with a plan to establish a commercial line
between Malaya and Japan. He, too, met with the still wealthy
and still disillusioned Anjiro. Alvaro told him of a wonder-
fully compelling Father Xavier who might perhaps find an
answer to his passionate questions and would certainly bring
light to his present gloom. Anjiro, having no occupation,
might have left at once, but he feared the long trip. One eve-

ning, however, in one of the dubious houses of the waterfront he killed a man, and the incident forced him to make the decision of which his unconstrained free will had been incapable. He took the first boat for Malacca, arriving there in 1546. Father Xavier had just left for the Moluccas.

Overwhelmed by disappointment and obedient to a fate which seemed to shape his condemnation, Anjiro bitterly left for home with no thought of the penalty awaiting him. For two years contrary winds tossed the melancholy young man about, until at the very end of the journey a chance storm drove him once more into port. To his surprise, he again encountered Alvaro Vaz, who reproached him for his indecision and transported him back to Malacca. Thus, after three sea-borne years of fearful, reticent, living hope, the man from Japan came to approach the apostle.

Francis had just finished presiding at a marriage ceremony— a true "reconciliation with God," for a Portuguese man was taking a slave to wife—when he observed the unfamiliar figure, a dark-skinned little man whose great saber kept hitting against one leg. Anjiro bowed low three times. Francis extended his hands—and Anjiro took them. In that quick second, Japan took Francis Xavier.

Francis left the church to talk with the young nobleman beneath a spreading tree. He was already won by the cultivated manner and intelligent eyes of this man from an unknown people; already he found Anjiro more worthy of esteem than even the Chinese. His melancholy was the dissatisfaction of a soul without God. Never was Francis so attentively heard, or by one more eager for his words and friendship. Anjiro made an attempt to remain politely inscrutable, but actually, his empty heart had filled. Francis wanted to give him his rosary. "But our women use them in the temples!" Anjiro exclaimed.

"Ah?" murmured the astonished Francis, and suddenly he decided to visit Japan and see for himself its subtlety of spirit and its customs akin to those of Christianity.

"I have looked long for you," said Anjiro.

"And I," thought Xavier, "was I not searching, too?"

Anjiro, who had at once asked for baptism, was taken before the Vicar of Malacca,[47] and subjected to a brusque interrogation:

"Married?"

"Yes."

"And returning to a pagan wife?"

"But . . ."

"Give up the idea of baptism."

Anjiro, his new faith dashed, complained to Francis, who, despite his concern, had determined never to interfere with the decision of ecclesiastical authorities who might crush him. Anjiro, reflecting on the strangeness of a faith preached by one so kind and another so hard, sank into fresh despair . . .

Francis sought to calm and pacify him, even allowing himself to become somewhat demonstrative towards this stoical Japanese. Anjiro could not have taken offense. He had, in his own words, "succumbed completely" to the other's charm. Navarre and the Orient, each correctly aristocratic, might still greet one another in style.

Francis kept the man with him for a week of instruction and, during the time, drew him out to speak of home and family, of friends and Japanese ethics. The apostle was developing something of a passion for the country which had sent him a son so spent with vicissitudes, so unhappy in his ignorance of God. The responsibilities of India, Malaya, and the Moluccas had been met. Off to the east lay great islands of unfortunate creatures, and Francis determined to go there. Anjiro prepared him for disappointment:

He told me [wrote Francis] that the inhabitants of this country would not readily become Christian but would first ask me many questions; and that, if I could both speak eloquently and live above reproach, the king, the nobles, and all others of quality might become Christians within half a year.

It was not to be that simple, as both well knew, but faith was their support; and in this cabin at Malacca, away from Ignatius and deprived of Favre, Francis came once again to learn the meaning of friendship. The rigors of his life had always opened up some happy moment: on Cape Comorin with the Brahman hermit; in San-Thomé before the tremendous tomb in its strangely appropriate surroundings of a humble refectory garden; in Malacca by lamplight—a holy light which, within a few short evenings, consumed the mothlike melancholy of a small Japanese with a heavy saber . . .

Anjiro was to return on board the ship of Alvaro Vaz, the Portuguese merchant who had first brought him to Malacca. Francis left shortly before, planning to precede his journey to Japan with a general inspection of India. The trip was long, but for such a man uneventful, although he relates that the entire cargo had to be jettisoned in order to lighten the ship during a storm. Having only one possession, his breviary, he cared little for the fate of such silken stuffs whose delicate splendor could not compare with the nuances and joys of a single thought.

In January 1548, faithful to a tradition, Francis stopped once more at Cochin. Only there, with a coil of rope as his chair and the ship's wine for refreshment, could he find proper inspiration for his voluminous letter to Rome.[48] Cochin had not seen him for three years. The curling hair was now completely white, the face even thinner; his feet tough, horny, and permanently impregnated with reddish soil. No one dreamed that this returnee was thinking only of departure.

On the Cochin waterfront, which Francis used as something of a coffee house, he unexpectedly encountered the aged Bishop of Goa, obliged by the death of his two vicars to complete pastoral visitations in person. Francis was distressed to learn that he would not find Miguel de Vaz, who had received him so well in 1542. The Inquisitor—to use the distinguished title finally won from Portugal—had been assassinated, and shock and grief had brought the death of the second vicar. Who was responsible? The possibilities were numerous: Jews, Arabs, Portuguese, or even—this the distraught and powerless bishop had suggested himself—some clergyman terrified by the rigors of a new tribunal.[49]

There were additional surprises: the viceroy was no longer the faithful Sousa but John de Castro, fresh from a fairly decisive victory over the Moslems. In short, there was no particular pleasure to be anticipated in this forthcoming stay at Goa without friends or support from top administrators, and with the Church in anarchy under the trembling hand of a prelate both sceptical and wholly discouraged.

Francis' letter to John III hints at this piteous state of affairs—an unskillful letter, in which, fearful of any dissolution of power, he goes so far as to place members of the Society at the service of high authority—a position which would render them understandably suspect.

Ten further letters were written to regular correspondents; then Francis descended by way of Cape Comorin to Manapad, returning directly from there to Goa. Anjiro had just arrived, and the Bishop at least had the joy of baptizing him with the name of Paulo de Santa Fé. The Vicar of Malacca could say no more. For Father Xavier, however, the fifteen months in India were nevertheless exasperating. His attraction for the future made such forced concentration on the past highly distasteful, yet he must visit all of the Christian faith, assign newly arrived Jesuits, and deal with many details of unfinished business. Seventeen Jesuits were at that time already resident in India, all of them more than curious to see Francis—some for the first time. He made trip upon trip: first towards Bombay, then in April to Cochin, and once again to Cape Comorin, where he assembled most of the missionaries for a meeting.

Returning directly to Goa, he was delighted to find his friend from Lisbon, Paul de Camerino, who introduced Cosmas de Torres, a thirty-eight-year-old priest from Barcelona. Torres, a tumbleweed of the Xavier type, was asking admission to the Society. He had wandered about the Pacific for ten years by way of Mexico, the Philippines, and the Caroline Islands. An eternal vagrant, and strongly drawn to one who had roamed more than he, he attached himself firmly to Francis, knowing, and with cause, that he might go far . . .

Francis inspected the College of Saint Paul and was deeply interested to find it a hive of Jesuit activity under the able direction of Paul de Camerino and several teaching Fathers. Then he left Goa to rejoin John de Castro, the new viceroy, in Bombay. Their second meeting, unlike the first, led happily to firm friendship, with Castro entreating Francis to help him meet the problems ahead by staying on through the rainy season in Goa. After accepting the invitation, Francis wrote to his friend Pereira:

I, too, would have been happy to see you before you left, and to confide to you a rich merchandise which the traffickers of China and Malacca hold in little esteem. It is called the human conscience.

For all his nervousness, four years before his death Francis was still ready to smile.

The viceroy died of malaria during that mournful rainy season, with Francis watching beside him in the sorrow of new-found affection. Afterwards, he sought distraction by returning to the College of Saint Paul, where he found more new developments. Simon Rodriguez, now Provincial of the Jesuits of Portugal and its colonies—and, in consequence, Xavier's direct superior—had sent out a young priest, who was under thirty, to join Paul de Camerino as first rector. Antonio Gomez, a swaggering young gentleman, while intelligent, was both obstinate and scornful—an admirable orator who admired his own words and respected no one else. A product of the Jesuit seminary in Coïmbra, he had outbluffed Rodriguez and had been sent to India with full confidence.

Gomez' first act was to threaten with explusion any student in Saint Paul's not born of Portuguese noblemen, thereby ruling out, in effect, all native Asians. His second threat was to send back to Portugal, in chains, any Jesuit who opposed his will. Francis, indignant, sought to have Gomez assigned to Ormuz; but Gomez, already more powerful in Goa than Francis himself, could not be dismissed. For the first time Father Xavier had encountered opposition from a member of the Society, and he was almost too astounded to react. He could do no more than abandon both college and teaching Fathers to the clutches of Gomez, withdrawing Paul de Camerino, who, until Francis' return from Japan, would be named "Superior of the Jesuits in India," i.e., Superior of Ormuz, Cape Comorin, and the Moluccas, but not of Goa. The compromise was neither satisfactory nor authoritative. Francis had behaved throughout the disagreement with such gentleness and patience, even lassitude, that Gomez prided himself on having the upper hand.

Arrivals in India had become more frequent, and now included Dominicans and, for the first time, Portuguese families. Among the Jesuits, Francis had the joy of encountering two after his own heart: Father Berze and Brother Juan Fernandez. Gaspar Berze, a Fleming, had studied at Louvain before entering the seminary in Coïmbra. He was an ardent, perceptive young man with a taste for adventure and a ready resistance to hardship. With sheets of water crashing upon the deck, he had blessed a storm. His sure judgment and absolute loyalty would be a frequent source of consolation. As for Fernandez, a rich young Cordovan, he was slender, refined, and somewhat affected, like one who sought to forget the premature pleasures his adolescence had brought him. He, too, would become a faithful follower, giving Xavier a devotion without reserve.

What might Ignatius think of this mission to Japan? Did Gomez' extended powers mean that he was even now to act in place of Francis? Had Ignatius, as André Bellessort seems to think, begun to lose confidence? The opinion is untenable.[50] While Ignatius might be annoyed to be henceforth out of touch with Francis' travels, he was not given to writing, and many Jesuits in India would have occasion to complain to Rome of being left constantly to themselves without directives.

XIII

In January 1549, Francis paid his regular visit to Cochin. There, kneeling on the ground with utter disregard for chains, wood fragments, and other debris of the waterfront, he wrote Ignatius that he was leaving for Japan. The letter is not without humor: "I could write you indefinitely of the inner consolations which come to me as I look ahead to this voyage so filled with the deadly perils of storms, winds, shoals, and pirates." Yet a note of sadness follows: "I so keenly hope, dear Father, that for one year you will ask some member of the Society, each month, to offer a Mass for me." From Cochin he returned to Goa, said his farewells, and set sail on April 15.

To sail eastward, for Xavier, was to meet the unknown. No cartographer, no historian had specified what might be found at the ends of the earth. Prevailing opinion saw Japan as a fragment detached from China; and Japan, moreover, was seen as comprising merely the southern portion of Honshu and Kyushu with its dusting of lesser islands. No one dreamed of an interlocking succession of islands and peninsulas forming an empire unknown to the West. Anjiro himself, though of a rich and cultivated family, knew only his own city of Kagoshima. The rest was as vague as drifting clouds.

The trip would be no gay excursion. Anjiro, thinking back over past perils, found the long crossing appealing only because of Francis' company. The man from Japan had learned

Portuguese during his year at Saint Paul and had, at Francis'
request, spent time in the college library transcribing the Gospel of Saint Matthew into Japanese. Francis himself had spent
some time practicing the calligraphy and even sent samples
to Ignatius, who was enchanted by the beauty of the little
symbols. In Rome the lovely and mysterious drawings went
from hand to hand, and Father Xavier seemed very learned
indeed.

During the first part of the trip he was accompanied by
Father de Torres and Brother Hernandez; Anjiro and two recently baptized Japanese domestics; two further converts, one
Chinese, one Hindu; and three Jesuits bound for the Moluccas, who went with them as far as Malacca.

The voyage was delightful. Francis had never known such
brilliant and cordial companionship, and never had he felt in
such good health. Contrary to all expectations, the winds were
mild and the weather fair for a peaceful cruise of relaxing,
calm days and intelligent discussion.

Malacca on May 31 was glorious. Everyone seemed to sense
the presence of a future saint and surrounded him with attention. The Captain, Pedro da Gama, a son of the famous
navigator and brother of Sousa's unhappy prisoner—was solic-
itous to the point of presenting Father Xavier with six tons
of pepper, a somewhat cumbersome fortune which Francis returned with instructions that it be sold and the proceeds
used to finance his mission. He sent final counsel to the
churches of India, while maintaining his check on the local
customs of Malacca—the city abounded, unfortunately, in
overwealthy merchants and women without means. Francis
became an inveterate matchmaker. "Here in Malacca," he
wrote with habitual mischievousness, "I encountered one of
my good friends, a bachelor in comfortable circumstances. I

spoke to him of a young lady whom I knew and whose vir-
tues I praised highly. He found both *the idea and the young
lady* attractive." Thus, he gave some equilibrium to this society so easily tempted to "keep" but not to wed . . .

Malacca and Francis once again became accustomed to one
another, since no captain was anxious to try his luck on a
trip to Japan, especially since the great Malay port, in losing
Father Xavier, would lose its central figure. Pedro da Gama
sought to intercede, but in vain, and Francis was finally
obliged to charter the great junk of a pagan pirate named
Ladrão, who was suspected of being a sea wolf. His wife and
property, both within the city, were seized and held by Pedro
da Gama against fulfillment of contract, with the property
representing more of a security than the wife.

On June 24 the junk set forth on its long journey. Pedro da
Gama, fearing that the Fathers were too naïve, had at the
last moment put one of his officers on board to keep watch
over the pirate. Ladrão was skillful as a pilot but mistakenly
guided in all important maneuvers by a wooden idol with
glittering glass eyes. The idol had been placed on the rear deck
where the sailors might prostrate themselves in veneration.

Francis had stocked the junk with riches that Ladrão might
well have found tempting: a portable chapel with costly ac-
cessories; gold; and rich materials, some of them destined for
the "king" of Japan. Since Da Gama's officer never took his
eyes from the pirate, the atmosphere on board was somewhat
strained. Ladrão, however, behaved decently enough and was
even, for Francis, an object of pity when a storm off the coast
of Cochin China swept his young daughter overboard in full
view of her father and the passengers. Birds of sacrifice were
offered before the idol, and the lamentations were prolonged
throughout one day and night.

Ladrão wished to winter off Canton but was compelled to

raise anchor and go on. Thus Francis, unsuspecting, passed by the site of his death. After other vicissitudes and endless discussions about direction, the stars being in disagreement with the idol, the junk reached Kagoshima on August 15, a date dear to Xavier for it had once marked the annual reunions of the original Iniguistas at the chapel on Montmartre.

The great junk caused excitement in the harbor of Kagoshima not only for its unusual shape, its silken cargo, and the white-robed strangers, who landed without firearms, but because it had brought back the nobleman Anjiro, whose face, while still wearing its customary passivity, was no longer veiled in sadness. He seemed more virile, and his curving saber had been replaced by the long straight blade of a sword. Francis immediately went in to Kagoshima, a large town surrounded by rolling hills, its clustering houses roofed with thatch or tiles. Straight rows of cherry and orange trees stretched away into the distance, while the lowlands held rice paddies, green rectangles of broken, mirrorlike reflections. It was the last and southernmost city of Japan—a lordly city mild in atmosphere, though occasionally vexed, as are all happy cities, by violent storms.

Francis and Anjiro learned quickly that the country was in a state of upheaval, with the princes at each other's throats. The usual royal pastime was in this instance fairly grave: the emperor was becoming senile and the princes were not puppets, as were the rajahs of India, but flesh and blood. The Portuguese soon discovered that in this country of reason and intelligence, cities were not open to colonization. They might absorb strangers but they would not admire them. The Japanese were highly literate people and the country was one of profound spirituality. The bonzes, or monks, were sages who were already familiar with the great seeds of universal wisdom. Their principles, however false, were free from any dross of ignorance. They were powerful, and on their power depended the unity of the country, transcending individual divisions and forming a general supreme force which could be neither purchased nor subjugated. Some of their monasteries were veritable fortresses where Japanese princes, victors and vanquished alike, found the same peaceful silence.

The bonzes of Kagoshima practiced Zen Buddhism, reserved for classes of superior culture, and combining the oddities and approximations of Taoism—Orientals like distinctive seasoning for both cooking and culture—with a Shintoism that was proud, stable, and reassuringly nationalistic.

It was understandable that the bonzes might look askance at the returning Anjiro. Francis Xavier could easily keep to the faith of his own country, but for Anjiro to have transferred his happiness from Buddhism to Christianity was unpardonable—and worse yet was the fact that he presented his wife and children for baptism. The delicate partitions of his house opened wide to the Jesuits. Never had Francis been received with greater delicacy or more discreet consideration. Whatever the difference between these slender panels of sliding wood and the thick walls of a Basque castle, Francis felt at home with an aristocratic family of duty—a family enjoying the extraordinary peace of local respectability. He had traveled over great oceans only to find the best of Europe, in intent if not in manner, on these farthest shores: ideas of dignity and liberty, of the superiority of good over evil, of well-doing over misdeed . . . Enchanted by the moderation and polish of these people, Francis gave himself for the moment to enjoying them. On all sides he found them reading and writing with meticulous ease, endowing every relationship with courtesy, loving and praising nature without quaking, face downward, in the presence of the elements. Rich and poor alike, in all their reactions, displayed an easy tranquility deriving from mastery of self. He tried to accustom himself to chopsticks and lacquer and the taste of saki. He paid and received innumerable calls with all the salutations of a pre-apostolate. He slept on a quilted matting which was rolled up by day and concealed in a closet. There where Christian prayer had been unknown, he prayed.

On his arrival, Anjiro had been summoned by the Daimyo of Kagoshima ("the Duke," wrote Francis, having his own concept of titles) to his palace some distance from the city. The Daimyo, curious to see his melancholy relative after so many years, could readily detect change and inner peace in the appropriately inscrutable countenance. Questioned on his travels and on the "Portuguese bonze," Anjiro described the glory of this foreigner, his reputation among kings and viceroys, the infinite charm of his conversation, the beauty of his faith. The Prince nodded; trade with Portugal was his favorite dream, and Francis would doubtless mention Kagoshima to powerful friends. Anjiro presented him with a painting of the Blessed Virgin; and the Prince, ever courteous, bowed low, calling upon his own mother to share in admiring this charming work of art. Anjiro left the palace much encouraged and began to give receptions in his home at which he explained the Christian religion and proposed group recitation of prayers which he had translated from Xavier's original texts. As the fire began to smolder, several of his friends were converted.

One month later, Francis was granted an audience at the palace, in itself something of a formidable stronghold, and worthy of this prince who was sixth in importance among the thirty-six daimyos of the Empire. Francis had stepped into a feudal system. The interview, in which he asked how best to reach the Emperor of Miyako,[51] was fairly short, and the Prince was evasive. He liked the European, however, and arranged that residence within the city be provided for him with free authorization to teach his religion. Francis proceeded accordingly, and the bonzes, seeing no danger, frequently exchanged visits with him. During these visits their dialogue continued—friendly, simple, and gratuitous, with neither party thinking of yielding an inch. This confrontation in the autumn setting of Kagoshima was interesting: two great religions of the heart faced one another—the only faiths that have helped tremendous populations to live without obsession and to die in hope. The exchange of words was frequently subtle.

"What period of life seems preferable to you," asked Xavier, "youth, or the advanced age to which you have now attained?"

"Youth," replied the bonze, "for the body is strong."

"What moment," Xavier continued, "is most favorable for those traveling from one port to another: is it found on the high seas, when one is exposed to the storms, or when the port of destination comes in sight?"

"For a man sure of his destination," said the bonze, "and sure of finding the harbor open, the best moment comes with his approach thereto; *but I know not where my ship is heading* nor how I shall reach the goal."

The most humble witness to these fresh and penetrating discussions was Francis' little Japanese servant, who knelt to serve their tea and later knelt in faith when she received the baptismal name of Mary. She was never to forget him, blessing her master while withstanding lengthy persecution from the bonzes, until at last, under the protection of the Japanese Jesuits, she died at an advanced age.

Winter came, and Francis rejoiced to see fresh changes of color in a world of nature which for eight years had seemed to him unvarying in its splendor. "The wild vines fall in wondrous scarves from the trees, and all of this Japan, heady with autumn, is filled with the airlike honey of the sun," writes Kikuo Yamata. Francis seized the moment to produce another voluminous missive—this time not to Ignatius but to the Fathers at Goa—filled with tales of travel, an introduction to the Japanese mentality, and a collection of excellent religious maxims. He dreamt of going to the Emperor of Japan, but no one would tell him the way. He dreamt of the great universities of the north as sites for a possible Jesuit college—unaware that these universities were actually monasteries. He dreamt of enclosing within a globe of Christianity these souls which—why not?—appeared to him as superior; yet, with the exception of a limited circle, he met only reserve. Finally—and here ended all his dreaming—he was beginning to plan a trip to China, that immense double purse almost within reach and overflowing with seed to be rooted in the good field.

Meanwhile he was wasting time. Now that the novelty of his presence had worn off, fewer Japanese came to see him; and Kagoshima, after all, was but a village. Cosmas de Torres and the gentlemanly Brother Fernandez, who had been completely won by Japanese civility, were learning the language of the country; but Francis' contacts were in the long run limited to those of his own rank. Among these were Ninjit, superior of the monastery of Kagoshima, who was an ironic and disillusioned nobleman for whom the Christianity of this grave and handsome foreigner supplied a tiny flame which might alone survive extinction within the rarefied atmosphere of his cell and his unhappy heart, and Nanjri, another influential bonze, who, although he was one of the most learned men of the Empire, felt deeply his ignorance of Christian writings. The interest of these men was, however, purely esthetic and their compromising meetings with Francis were veiled in secrecy. After one year, the Christian community in

Kagoshima numbered no more than one hundred persons. Francis regretted this deeply, for, as all his letters attest, he admired the Japanese sense of honor and their respect for the poor. For the first time in the Orient he had encountered kindred souls, and, determined to supplement his attempts at Christian penetration, he called on Father Berze to come and join him.

At the end of the year Francis decided on a trip to Hirado, an island port near the upper coast of Kyushu. Here the Portuguese had established headquarters for their commerce with Japan because the roads of Hirado seemed vaster than those of Kagoshima. The journey would be on foot, for Ladrão had died suddenly at Kagoshima. Francis' departure was encouraged by the Daimyo, who hoped to obtain publicity for Kagoshima as well as the possible transfer of the Portuguese shipping installations.

To cross Kagoshima and locate a junk in which to reach Hirado required two weeks. Historians tend to depict the apostle's long march through the interior as extremely difficult, but actually he must have found it very interesting. Up to now in Japan he had known but one harbor town; now he was getting acquainted with the land and its proud and modest people. Unlike men of the sea, these people were more firmly and genuinely rooted in tradition. They were independent and, despite their poverty, showed no greed. Francis observed. This southern part of the Empire was quite thickly settled and in the course of history would become one of the most populated areas.

He saw the subtlety of their medical practice illustrated by a physician determining the organic disorders of his patient by taking the pulse count for half an hour, an hour, or as long as necessary. He witnessed a trial at which the defendant, condemned to death, was accorded the sympathetic and considerate favor of having his head removed by none but the closest relative. On all sides he received a friendly welcome, the impassive faces betraying no sign of surprise at seeing their fields crossed for the first time by a white man.

No letters awaited Francis at Hirado, and he left his own communications with the Portuguese. The lord of the region turned out to be a young pirate—one must make a living—who was hoping to secure a fortune through trade with the Portuguese. As a result, he saw no problem in having his people venerate the God of the "southern barbarians"—his harbor, his heart, his credit were all at their disposal.

Francis decided to take advantage of these good intentions, for when he returned to Kagoshima, he realized immediately that things were no longer flourishing and that the city had reached its full total of conversions. Accordingly, he decided that the center of the Jesuit efforts should be transferred to Hirado, and began the preparations. He rested for a time in the palace of Niiro Ise-No-Kaminodo, one of the Daimyo's more important vassals. This Samurai, sensing with deep affection Francis' goodness and strength of character, presented his wife, children, and servants for baptism, but he himself refused because of his position.

These moments of austere "palace life" were a rare form of respite in Father Xavier's existence. He talked with his host, played with the children, accepted saki proffered by a kneeling wife, and his cassock was washed and pressed. His smile on those about him brought God as an extra guest to the table of the Samurai. The former professor of philosophy, who had so often explained the meaning of life, now found himself listening agreeably to other explanations, which were perhaps lacking in truth but not in beauty or grandeur.

The Daimyo, meanwhile, felt that he had been deceived. Far from encouraging Portuguese trade, Francis now seemed ready to withdraw, and had moreover made some ill-chosen remarks on morals in the course of a recent visit with the bonzes. In a country where women were considered as chattels and where orange-robed communities of priests knew no distraction, sodomy was prevalent, permissible, and respected —the women themselves admitted that their poor persons could be of no use. Francis, in a final and friendly effort towards reform, had seriously offended the bonzes and made only enemies. This hostility, however, fell less upon him than on the Christians of Kagoshima, who, after his departure, were treated like social outcasts. Anjiro, mild interlocutor of the evenings in Malacca, would be scorned, ruined, and completely discredited, finally becoming a pirate and meeting death in a skirmish with Chinese fishermen. Francis and Anjiro wept as they parted; and neither knew for what reason . . .

A junk was supplied for the trip by the Daimyo of Kagoshima, who was most anxious to be rid of the troublemakers. Bloody linen had even been cast at their door one night to lend credence to an accusation of cannibalism. The Jesuits left Kagoshima and sailed up the coastline of Kyushu past Nagasaki. From there, rounding a hill heavy with underbrush, they reached the waters of Hirado.

XIV

Autumn, 1550. The brown sails of the junk were enthusiastically greeted with cheers and a cannonade from the Portuguese. Flags were run up quickly. Francis was becoming accustomed to these warm and promising arrivals. If the departures could but correspond . . . The cannonade had the triple effect of doing honor to the apostle, providing the Portuguese, even those awakened from a siesta, with a real distraction, and impressing the Japanese. The young lord of Hirado descended his palace steps to bow low before the tall man in white.

Within two months one hundred Japanese had been baptized in Hirado—a total reached in Kagoshima only after a year of residence. The elegant Brother Fernandez, who had replaced Anjiro as interpreter, strove to outdo his interlocutors with courteous and polished phrases, extending the arms of an archangel over their fixed and shining eyes.

Father Xavier was lodged with a certain Kimura, who proved no more resistant to conversion than any previous host and who was the first in Hirado to ask for baptism.[52] Despite this encouraging start, however, and regardless of the young nobleman's outstretched hand, Francis had no intention of lingering on a little island which would inevitably prove to be a repetition of Kagoshima. With the approach of winter, he put Cosmas de Torres in charge of the group. Then, accompanied by Brother Fernandez and a pious Japanese servant, he left.

The journey led them first by sea to the tip of the great island of Honshu, from which they thrust inland over vast territories seemingly shredded from the Empire and extending it to the west—"at the limit," to use humorless geological terms, "of one of the most sunken portions of the earth's crust."[53] Although all three were accomplished horsemen, they now had to advance on foot through unfamiliar territory and without a map, ignorant of what lay around them. The cold descended. Mountains, valleys, and roads were covered with snow. They had only one blanket among them and took turns carrying a bundle which contained Francis' surplice, his shirts, and the vessels used for Mass. Covered with mud, driven from the inns, and stoned by children, they continued their imperturbable way. Their only food was fried rice, for Francis had become a vegetarian out of deference to the bonzes, for whom all life is sacred.[54]

Of all Father Xavier's journeys, this was the most arduous, and a rude initiation for Fernandez, who recounts, "Mountains and valleys were but snow to the eye. Nothing round about us brought relief." The western coast of Japan is exposed to winds from Siberia, but Francis bore with its rigors, moving pitifully forward, moving on in prayer. The small volume of Ignatius had been his training, and his eyes were closed to what lay ahead. The countryside lay within him. He was not frozen; his soul was on fire.

Paradoxically, the snow which covered the roads that year was an advantage, for it interrupted the civil war in which the island was involved, and obliged each faction to seek winter quarters. Otherwise, Francis would never have reached his destination. Three people, including an aged Samurai, were baptized in the course of that journey, which brought the Jesuits at long last to Yamaguchi, an important city of ten thousand houses surrounded by bald hilltops, and ruled by one of the mightiest daimyos of the Empire.

Father Xavier had no thought of remaining in Yamaguchi, however, but planned simply to catch his breath there while awaiting an opportunity to head for Miyako, the imperial city which for two years had been the object of his dreams. But after a few days, rest became unbearable, and posting himself on street corners with Fernandez, he taught the Gospel to astonished residents, some of whom openly made fun of him until they were silenced by a glance from Francis, who brooked no resistance and commanded self-abasement. Prominent persons received him into their homes, seated him on leopard skins, and served him tea. His own host, Uchida, inevitably presented himself and his wife for baptism.

An audience with the powerful Daimyo, however, brought only disaster. Received most courteously at first in a palace hall reserved for ambassadors, they were questioned by the Prince as to their identity, their travels, and finally, their religion. Fernandez, at Francis' signal, began to read from a small volume which Francis had written. When he decried sodomy as displeasing to God, the Prince—understandably—became infuriated and motioned the "ignorant" strangers from the room. Francis made a dignified exit, insisting vainly, but as a matter of form, on the excellence of what had just been read. "I myself was afraid he would take off our heads," wrote Fernandez.

No second bidding was needed. Francis and his modest following withdrew from Yamaguchi. In this week before Christmas, the snow lay thicker than ever, and with every step they sank to their knees, arriving after great difficulty at their port of embarkation, the harbor of Iwahuni on the Inland Sea. A trip through this immense, island-studded canal gave promise of being pleasant in spite of a heavy mist which seemed at sunset to hang from the rigging in clusters of rosy globes. Unfortunately, the boat was filled with boors who took offense at the distinguished manner of the saintly traveler and persecuted him unmercifully. At one of the stops a Buddhist savant, moved to pity, supplied the three strangers with a letter of introduction to a friend in the port of Sakai, just beyond Osaka.

Sakai proved to be a rich and stately city of such size that the three wanderers were quickly lost, and, since no one would direct such disreputable characters, it was not until the following day that they located the house of the wealthy merchant to whom they had been recommended. The merchant fed and clothed them, presenting Francis with a superb turban which the apostle promptly put on his head, and which apparently gave him quite an air.

With hot water, abundant food, and a quilted sleeping mat, Francis recovered his youthful exuberance. The merchant, meanwhile, discovered a means of getting them to Miyako by having them enrolled as domestics in the service of a prince traveling to the Imperial City by palanquin. Thus it happened that two Jesuits—one an apostle and a papal nuncio— laden with royal luggage, trotted along barefoot behind the drawn curtains of a sumptuous litter. Francis found the distasteful situation highly amusing, and, according to Fernandez, pranced ahead like a happy child. Thus Father Xavier, bearer of Christ, entered Miyako—the Kyoto of today—the largest and most beautiful city in Asia.[55]

Geographically, Miyako was similar to Paris. Each of its innumerable straight avenues led directly to a monastery, one of which, Hiei-Zan, was perched on an elevation and constituted, in a sense, the Sorbonne of the city. Francis would quickly learn that admittance was not to be easily gained.

Kyoto and Florence have marked similarities [writes Fosco Maraini]. Each city, for its respective continent, has been a guardian to lofty traditions of the mind; and, although the Arno valley is less broad than that of the Kamogawa, there is a certain physical similarity as well . . . Florence and Kyoto are essentially two agglomerations spreading over a plain hemmed in by hills and mountains . . . The very dialects present similar phenomena, such as a tendency to aspiration. Why should Kyoto be thus captivating, as a city with a soul, a message, and a unique personality? Why not a mere site or chapter in the history of twenty-six civilizations? In Kyoto all is refined rather than useful . . . yet Florence is the West, gleaming in beauty, a potion to be drained from the magic cup. Kyoto is the East—mysteriously beautiful, slowly won . . . all its treasures stored in the green cradles of its valleys, within the folds of its hills, while the city itself could be roughly divided into two zones: a girdle of wooded hills and lakes, of scattered temples, cities, gardens, monasteries, and hermitages—a crown of ascetic delights with the city as its center.[56]

In any case, Fosco Maraini's Kyoto is identical with that of Xavier. As in the beautiful Tuscan city of Florence, time has altered neither plan nor charm nor spirit.

A certain Ryusa was Francis' host, but unlike his other hosts, the light of Grace would come belatedly to him some ten years later. Francis made prompt but vain attempts to obtain access to the monastery of Hiei-Zan: heavy walls kept all but nobles and purveyors of costly gifts from gaining admittance to the three thousand temples and seminaries of what Francis called the "university." Disconsolate at finding no door after several rounds of the enclosure, Father Xavier returned to the city and went to the Imperial Palace. There

again, however, payment had to be made. Moreover, it was
rumored that the pathetic Emperor, revered but powerless
within his bamboo palisade, was trying to market his own
poems as a means of livelihood. Surrounded by prostrate
subjects who brought him no rice, he was dying of boredom
and of hunger. For a gift of rice, if he had dared, Francis
might perhaps have gained admittance. He had learned, however, that Japanese administration was not like that of Spain,
and after eleven days of impatient scuffling, he withdrew from
the capital. The great journey had resulted in total failure: the
Emperor had given no permission to preach the Gospel
through the Empire, and Fernandez had not been allowed to
observe in the university. But despite his great disappointment, Francis admired the great city. He had also been the
first white man to enter Miyako, the heart of the Nipponese
Empire.

March 1551. Francis and Fernandez landed in Hirado and
met an overjoyed Cosmas de Torres, who had never thought
he would see them again. They were depressed by their unsuccessful mission, but they at least had seen the most beautiful city of the Orient.

But was the mission a failure? Later Jesuits arriving in Sakai
and Miyako would find courage and extraordinary inspiration
in following Father Francis. [Although he had come too late
to an ancient civilization, yet life, within old age, ferments
anew and calls for renewal. From this ebullient change would
come a modern world, a modern spirituality, a living love of
Saint Francis.]

In any case, he had understood Miyako. He learned that
the most powerful warrior of the Empire, with authority even
over the Emperor himself, was none other than the Daimyo
of Yamaguchi, who would so willingly have had their heads.

The next step would be a farce. Since the University and palace had been mockingly closed to him because of his wretched appearance, he would take advantage of the senseless superiority of the well-dressed man. Francis Xavier, who, in his youthful capitulation to Ignatius, had abandoned cloaks, collars, and doublets, now dipped into the treasure he had intended for the Emperor. Under Fernandez' critical eye for Old-World elegance, he tried on silken robes and selected costumes.

When all was ready, Francis, Juan Fernandez, and two Christian domestics set sail from Hirado. Sailing across the Inland Sea, they put into the port of Mitajiri, a great luxurious city at the head of a valley. In Mitajiri they rented horses and—lest things be done halfway—a palanquin for Francis. Then they made a sensational entry into Yamaguchi.

The palace doors opened promptly for these fine lords. The Daimyo found it difficult to recognize these two "barbarians," who wore their splendid clothes with such an air, as the ragged priests of the last visit. Father Xavier looked as though he had stepped from a tapestry and, for once, resembled the cards, ceramics, and frescoes of future religious art. We may laugh at him—the joke is easily shared—but the honors and consideration had been richly earned: silk for a skin burned by nine years of sun and snow, boots for feet constantly bare, fresh golden cloth for a feverish head, brocaded gloves for hands that had been spread to cover so many lost souls with the protection of baptism . . .

The admiring Daimyo called for a carpet to provide rest for Lord Francis and his dapper secretary, but they did not rest. Instead, Xavier had his two servants unwrap several presents: a clock that struck the hours; a music box; a mirror —though, alas, the Daimyo had no wives; a three-barreled musket; several lengths of brocade; two pairs of spectacles;

finely bound books; fine crystal; and kegs of port. Even without partaking of this last, the Prince was staggered. Although he was a wealthy advisor to the Emperor and master of much of the insular territory, he had never seen or possessed such marvels. Drawing himself up for a speech of acceptance, he was cut short by Francis, who produced various documents: credentials from John III, the "barbarian" king; from the Bishop of Goa; and from the Pope, Paul III.

The stage had been fully set—yet actually, no "stage" was required. The apostolic nuncio had presented himself with the normal train of a European diplomat visiting the Orient. Needless to say, the Prince granted Francis' every wish; and, not to be outdone, presented him with a bag of gold, his admiration reaching new heights when the former refused to accept it. By royal command, printed notices were publicly displayed which authorized the Christian religion to be taught and freely accepted within the Empire; and to cap the climax, Francis was presented with a monastery. At long last a gemlike little palace had provided a roof for his head.

Francis had many callers during the "folly" of Yamaguchi. All the nobility, in imitation of their prince, came to hear him; and, after them, the people of the town. Slowly but surely came sensational conversions; and in the once hostile city, Francis now made staunch friends. Rigid social systems can leave one to walk unknown and stoned among persons who, looking, might come to love. Wealth and acclaim establish friendships because they bring communication.

Many of Francis' new Christians were members of prominent local families for whom a mere catechism could not suffice. There were grave discussions. The Japanese, astonished by Christian concepts of good and evil, were entitled to an explanation:

"We told them there was but one principle, completely good, unmixed with evil."

"But what of wicked devils, enemies of the human race?"

"God created them good; they brought evil upon themselves."

Such discussions elicited one comment reported by Francis to Ignatius: "They say that their laws are much more firmly rooted in compassion than the laws of God."

The fact that the Buddhists of the hundred temples of Yamaguchi, unlike the Zen Buddhists of Kagoshima, believed in the soul's immortality served somewhat to reconcile the two theses.

Francis was exposed to a battery of questions for which answers were occasionally difficult. Buddhism is a religion of philosophers, polishing time-honored truths as the sea smooths its rounded pebbles, reflecting sagely on each article from one century to the next. Xavier, however, was his own answer, in himself a reflection of God. Strong men capitulated to the light in his eyes rather than to the awkward and necessarily sketchy nature of his teaching. Fernandez' lessons in Japanese had not made him fluent, and the dialect of Yamaguchi was not that of Kagoshima . . .

Yet, after all, Francis' success in this brilliant city was perhaps based on esteem. Five hundred people were baptized in six months—a modest total for sizable Yamaguchi, the second largest city of Japan. Francis was far from satisfied and apparently left the monastery by night to continue his discourse from a well curb in the center of a square. Historians draw a sentimental parallel between Xavier in Yamaguchi and Jesus at Jacob's well. The simple fact, however, was that Francis could be sure of an audience at a spot where great numbers of women and children gathered to draw water for the evening meal. These lamplit evenings had a certain poetic charm as winds from the valley ruffled the apostle's gleaming silken robe and, close at hand, a young wandering minstrel, something of an oriental troubadour, sang sweetly to the strains of his own guitar. This charming half-blind boy would one day be a Jesuit, wandering, guitar in hand, to take his glowing faith about the countryside. He would appeal to many souls, take issue with many bonzes. "Thou wilt quickly learn if the soul be immortal!" howled a Zen Buddhist, saber in hand, on one dramatic occasion—but the weapon remained suspended before the literally disarming smile of the one-eyed Jesuit. A slender thread of happiness, in a sense God's ratification of the work Francis was completing, ran through these days, and without it the weary apostle might not have been able to push on.

It was time to leave Yamaguchi, and the departure was climaxed by the momentous baptism of a great scholar, a specialist in Confucianism and a sage whose words carried particular weight throughout the province. The effect was far-reaching, yet the majority of this society, too sophisticated for such "infatuations," remained unmoved.

Rather than leave this Christian community to itself, Francis had Cosmas de Torres come from Hirado to take charge. Fernandez would stay with him. Father Xavier then said good-bye to the Prince who had so freely opened the doors of his palace. Such ready cordiality, with that of other lords and Buddhist dignitaries, had been of great advantage to Francis, for whom the months in Yamaguchi might count among the most sociable of his life. He had talked much and listened much, with no previous knowledge of Buddha, and he had received a detailed Japanese explanation of Buddhism.

In mid-September of 1551 he left with three domestics for Bungo, a small principality on the great island of the south. There he was received by an amiable and childlike daimyo

who was something of a pirate and whose harbor was tem-
porarily occupied by a Portuguese ship under Duarte da Gama,
whom Francis knew. After a royal welcome and a stop to
hear confessions on the Portuguese ship, an ornately trimmed
boat, its brilliant sails filling in the wind, took Francis to
a neighboring port where the Daimyo had organized a fes-
tival in his honor. The two men liked one another, and Francis made several conversions in the entourage of the Prince,
who, without committing himself, was favorably inclined towards the Christian religion.[57]

Father Xavier, however, was hardly in a mood for discussions. He was deeply disturbed that Duarte da Gama had
brought him no mail. For more than two years he had been
without news from Rome and India. What had happened?
Gravely concerned, he wrote Cosmas de Torres not to expect
him in Yamaguchi; he would try to reach Malacca and India,
not returning to Japan until the following year.

Just as he was on the point of leaving, a letter from Cosmas de Torres brought shocking news. A vassal of the Daimyo
of Yamaguchi had invaded, pillaged, and burned the town,
and the Daimyo, draining a last glass of Francis' port, had
killed his son and fallen on his own sword to avoid capture.
The Christians had been mistreated and scattered, with Torres
and Fernandez escaping to take refuge with a learned friend.
Once new authority was firmly established, the imperturbable Torres had promptly claimed damage and interest for
the sacked and ruined monastery of the Jesuits.

Nothing, however, was irreparable, and through a diplo-
matic move encouraged by Francis, the brother of his host
was soon named Daimyo of Yamaguchi. Father Xavier
thought compassionately of the perverse but well-meaning
prince who had found suicide essential. But the situation was,
after all, well under control, since the throne of the famous

city would be occupied by a close relative[58] of a prince already receptive to Christianity.

Francis set sail, supported by the presence of a royal ambassador sent to the Viceroy of the Indies. The trip was frightful. Seven days out of Japan, the ship was caught in a typhoon and sucked into a terrifying whirlpool. When it was finally cast out, it was lost among the Indonesian archipelagos. During the storm, the captain, to lighten the boat, had put two sailors with a few biscuits into a small skiff riding astern. The rope gave way, but the sailors were found safe and sound three days later. Francis had spent the time in prayer.

On December 17, badly damaged and with its sails in shreds, the ship entered the Bay of Canton and dropped anchor off Sancian Island. There Francis had a joyful reunion with Diego Pereira, his friend from Cochin. Together, they strolled up and down the beach, looking out over the Bay with its red- or black-sailed junks departing for Canton. Suddenly, Francis felt the call of China. He had plowed a Christian furrow through the multiple Indies and the many islands of Japan. And China? Silently, Pereira listened, little knowing what the year would bring.

Pereira's ship, the *Santa Cruz*, took Francis to Singapore. He was perfectly at home on the ship for these good days of perfect friendship beneath a blue sky, and there was much to discuss. On Christmas day in 1551 they reached Singapore with its great white cathedral; and on that Christmas night— his last—the great white figure of Francis Xavier, his heart singing, stood by the waterfront.

XV

There were reddish slashes through the forest of masts in the harbor of Malacca such as one sees after a forest fire in Provence. Some of the boats had capsized. The Malay sultans' attempt to reclaim the city had failed, but only after a heated contest. Nevertheless, Malacca gave Francis an affectionate welcome, and Father Perez, the priest in charge, resisted his own ill-health to arrange that Francis be carried in procession up to the lofty church. He also gave him a packet of letters bearing various dates, one of which apprised Francis of his appointment by Ignatius de Loyola as Provincial of the Society of Jesus for the Indies "and countries beyond." The responsibility was obviously weighty—the term "Indies" comprised all countries from western Africa to southeastern Asia, and "beyond" was evidently a reference to China and Japan. Thus freed from the somewhat ponderous supervision of Simon Rodriguez, Francis found himself with full authority and a new task as administrator general of the missions.

Still accompanied by the Japanese ambassador and his almond-eyed servants, Francis embarked for India, reaching Cochin on January 24, 1552. The new viceroy, Alfonso de Noronha, proved obliging but somewhat indifferent. Francis had let himself be forgotten.

A tradition is a tradition. Once again in Cochin, Father

Xavier settled down to correspondence, each letter almost a book in itself. He gave an account of his journey through Japan, becoming almost poetic in his love for these difficult and appealing souls; he announced his imminent departure for China; and accepted under obedience the position of Provincial. "I had hoped that you would confide me to the Society, and not the Society to me," he wrote to Ignatius; then, amid passing stevedores and bibulous sailors, and surrounded by gaping crates, he yielded to reverie. "My heart has been filled with memories of other days," he went on. "I thought of the great love which Your Charity bore for me and bears me still." Then follows the disenchanted signature, "Your least of sons, and, of all, the one most exiled, Francis." A concise and affectionate word went also to the Fathers in Europe.

"In exile . . . ," yet Ignatius had authorized and even commanded his return to Rome. Eleven years had passed since the *Santiago* had left Lisbon, and the Jesuit general preferred that Francis leave for Europe rather than China. With the new Pope, he felt it urgent and vital to receive a full oral account of the progress of the Society in India.

Francis, however, dismissed the idea, not absolutely—he would see—but as out of the question for the moment. The refusal shows to what extent he was obsessed with the idea of completing his exploratory mission. The East was calling for him: instructions must be given to the Fathers in India, errors put right, a common plan established. The exile would remain in exile, far from Ignatius' paternally extended hand —while the hand itself would be surely withdrawn in vexation.

Francis had now but a few months to live. Much work remained before the greatest adventure, but there would be no further joy. No day appeared to him a fruit for tasting, a sweet to the mouth; nor would he smile. He was becoming increasingly nervous, passing abruptly from sharpness to tears, although he retained his determination.

He arrived at Goa just in time. Antonio Gomez, who had already revealed something of his true colors before Francis' departure, had subsequently achieved a marked cleavage among the Fathers of India. As a "courtier-Jesuit" he had aligned himself so successfully with Portuguese of importance —the aged bishop, the new vicar, and anyone of note—that the remaining Fathers, inadequately protected by Paul de Camerino, were being constantly humiliated, persecuted, and held in check.

Gomez had made several blunders. A spacious Jesuit seminary erected at Cochin had simply assumed within its walls the church of the Brothers of Mercy. The results were far from good, and though Francis immediately restored the church to its owners, there was no way to remove it from within the seminary walls. At the College of Saint Paul, which Gomez had sought to transform into a colonial Coïmbra, all Asian students had been dismissed, leaving it a "rich kids'" establishment and Goa's most select school. Francis, angry, reintegrated the Asian inhabitants and endeavored to give a spirit of modesty to the students on whom he counted to form a future basis for Christian India. He also appointed and firmly supported a new rector, Father Barreto, whom he had summoned from Europe the previous year with this position in mind. Mortally offended, Antonio Gomez retired, it appears, for a vacation near Ceylon, where the princes of the area made mild sport of him but from which he returned with new strength. He was essentially good-hearted, and would have excelled as the prelate of a large capital, an extraordinary orator whose thundering and grandiose eloquence could draw universal tears. Having strayed into the Society of Jesus, however, he mistakenly preferred himself to Francis, whom he considered something of a visionary. In the middle of February, Francis received him at Goa—an interview shrouded in such complete mystery that the very name of Gomez seems to have disappeared from the annals of the times. In all probability there was an exchange of bitter words whereby Gomez overstepped his position and Francis took offense. The result was that Father Gomez, stripped of his titles, was sent into exile on the small island of Diu off Bombay—an island topped by a Portuguese fortress and in its way a hopeless Monte Cristo. Not content with removing the unfortunate braggart, Francis instructed Father Berze, second in authority, that should Gomez attempt to escape from Diu, he was to be automatically dropped from the Society. While these secret directives were not unknown to the prisoner, he nevertheless attempted a surreptitious departure for Rome shortly thereafter, hoping to appeal directly to Ignatius. That his ship went down en route is a sorry ending charged by many to the memory of Francis Xavier—yet there could have been no better. Ignatius would not have questioned the decisions of his personal representative. Gomez had displayed rage, disobedience, profound scorn for native inhabitants, and open resistance to a papal legate. His words with Francis had doubtless been cruel and chosen to wound: "evading responsibilities," "always elsewhere," "too ready to leave."

Two additional Fathers, Manuel de Morais and Francisco Goncalvez, received, with Gomez, the thunder of Francis' wrath. Having found their assignment in the Moluccas unbearable, they had vanished into thin air to enjoy the pleasures of the town, and the Provincial gave them no quarter. Both were dismissed from the Society and forbidden all contact with its members. "It was a heavy grief that I must needs send them home," wrote Francis, adding the dread sentence: "Worst of all, I fear they are not alone . . ."

Francis was beside himself, hardly recognizable as one who had been so patient with a doltish Mansilhas; so ready to embrace all headhunters of the island of Mora; and a close friend to Anjiro, the assassin. A Provincial, however, is not a wheelwork but a mainspring. The hierarchy of the Society is monarchic in inspiration, and the Provincial, within his own area, carries absolute authority.

Father Xavier spent two months at Goa—no longer as an apostle but as administrator of the missions, dictating a weighty correspondence to all Fathers in the Orient, outlining responsibilities, defining the limits of each, issuing general instructions . . . keenly active. For the first time, as administrator, he displayed a fine kinship with Ignatius, scribbling reams to go forth in all directions over his signature as marvels of lucidity, tact, and style. The correspondence is comparable to that of Napoleon for its tone of authority, its refusal to be blind, curt, or overkind.

Francis now appeared as a leader, yet the work brought no joy . . . His companions must first be firmly roused to action; and while the outstanding success of Cape Comorin was comforting, elsewhere things were different; India remained restive and disappointing. There are certain geological strata through which water will not pass, and the Christian faith had come quickly to bedrock. Francis called for loving perseverance.

Father Gaspar Berze, previously summoned to Japan, had found a substitute to replace him at Ormuz and was preparing to leave for the great islands of the East. Francis stopped him; Torres would do. He named Berze Vice-provincial to replace Father Barreto as the new rector of Saint Paul and sent the latter out to the crowded mission of Bas-

sein beyond Goa. Berze accepted these gifts with some mis-
givings and in consternation at the thought of Francis'
departure. The apostle, although still young, was emaciated;
his gaze was penetrating, yet his hair was completely white.

Somewhat feebly, Francis put all in order: Gomez was
subdued, the unruly priests removed from the Moluccas, all
missions organized into a working whole. Francis left an
envelope of documents thick as a testament but assembled
the priests of Goa for a last nocturnal meeting—a strange
night watch with the shadow of the Provincial extended on
the wall behind him and transforming him into the subject
of a picture.

Diego Pereira had received from the viceroy the title of
ambassador which Francis had declined for himself, and the
two men embarked on the *Santa Cruz* in April 1552. Francis was far from lighthearted. "When shall we meet Your
Reverence again?" cried one of the faithful from the receding
shore. And Francis, standing on the deck, called back, "In
the valley of Josaphat."

He was accompanied by several domestics—among them a
Chinese, Antonio, who had spent eight years at the College
of Saint Paul, and a Hindu, Christopher. With Pereira was
the Japanese ambassador from Bungo, who had been baptized
in Goa. Lastly, several Jesuits assigned to Malaya were to go
part way with their leader.

In addition to brocades, rugs, and other gifts, Xavier carried
with him for this trip a portable pontifical chapel, which
could be folded, unfolded, and set up in the manner of a
camping tent. With all safely stowed, and watched by only
a few spectators, the boat weighed anchor.

Cochin was an indispensable stop. Final letters were written, and then on April 24 the sails swelled in departure for Malacca. When the accustomed storm descended, the pontifical

chapel, with the rest of the cargo, was consigned to the deep, and the ship, thus lightened, reached the harbor of Malacca in May. Immediately on landing, Francis found himself unfortunately face to face with Alvaro da Gama, the same man who had spent several months of chained meditation in the hold of the *Coulam*. Alvaro was now Grand Captain of the port of Malacca; and Pedro da Gama, who had financed the entire Japanese venture so generously, was completely supplanted as captain of the city of this embittered brother.

Alvaro held his vengeance ready. Francis, up to now, in all his travels through dangerous ports, had escaped any underhanded fray, but now the time had come. Alvaro da Gama, respecting neither God nor the devil, had an account to settle. He began by refusing admittance to the *Santa Cruz* and wresting from Pereira his official documents—a merchant, he sneered, is no ambassador. Then, rallying Malacca's underworld, he aroused the city against Father Xavier. The favored town where Francis had known such joy now made him a stranger. On the orders of the Grand Captain, stones were thrown—darkly red volcanic stones whose color would have remained unchanged for having gashed the forehead of a saint.

Francis would not forgive. Several letters contain verbal lashings of Alvaro.[59] He retaliated with his authority as nuncio by issuing a decree of excommunication against Da Gama and called for the immediate departure of all Jesuits from Malacca. Alvaro, unmoved, spat before the vicar who had come to intercede in the name of justice. If Francis ever knew a keen dislike, it was for Alvaro da Gama, who, feeling himself the black sheep of the family, had held the world responsible. Resistance, however, was useless. Pereira remained under surveillance in Malacca; and Francis, seeing the failure of the embassy, decided to leave. The ship had previously been loaded with soldiers in the pay of Alvaro; and now the expedition, consisting only of Francis, a Jesuit, Ferreira, and the domestics Antonio and Christopher, with neither baggage nor official pretext for entry into China, set forth in gloom.

The voyage was lengthened by the captain's unfamiliarity with the waters. Francis, familiar with navigation, was obliged to act as pilot while the captain, in vexation, obeyed directions. Another enemy for Francis. It was the end of September before the *Santa Cruz*, having first described several circles about the spot in order to preserve the captain's honor as an independent, finally dropped anchor off Sancian Island in the Bay of Canton.[60] The island was sinister, covered only by brambles, its small bays concealing smuggler craft that ran contraband between China and the "southern barbarians." These smugglers were its only inhabitants, who, when they left, always burnt the little cabins they had constructed as they awaited the "lucky break." The Portuguese, delighted by the saint's arrival, offered him a hut and constructed a chapel of leafy fronds close by the water's edge. Looking out towards Canton through the mauve twilight, Francis remembered his last visit here with Pereira and their mutual hopes. The wind was pushing innumerable junks across the Bay. Close at hand, beyond that screen of light, lay China, and the beginning of another life . . .

Father Xavier offered Mass in his leafy chapel, heard confessions, and cared for the sick as well as the children who came running from idle boats to be with him. Occasionally, in the dark of night, a cargo was loaded, a cabin flamed, and a boat slipped out towards the high seas. Francis tried to find some Chinese who might surreptitiously get him to Canton. But any smuggler risked his life, and although, with strong oarsmen, a nocturnal crossing was possible, no one came forward. Francis resorted to drastic methods, and gave a considerable sum of money to a Chinese—who never reappeared thereafter—while the Portuguese warned him against dealing with fishermen who might set forth at sunset only to turn out the passenger's pockets and drop him overboard before arrival.

Boats withdrew from the island, each according to the success of its dealings. Every morning one less lay in the waters off Sancian; and through the early dawn Francis would follow the irrevocable disappearance of these floating fortresses turreted with sheets and rigging, the great brown helm raised as a hand in farewell. The *Santa Cruz*, obviously of no help, was now the only vessel on the horizon, and he was at swords' points with the captain—if indeed Francis had ever drawn a weapon other than the sword of the spirit . . .

In November another ship, leaving Sancian, carried his last letters. From this desert where nothing had value he now proposed a fabulous two tons of pepper—a fortune, but not enough—against passage to China. The atmosphere became charged and tense: for reasons unknown, Francis dismissed from the Society his companion, Brother Ferreira, who sheepishly returned to the *Santa Cruz*. Less determined than Father Xavier, he had doubtless been urging departure. Francis continued his correspondence with a letter to Pereira on November 12: "All my life I shall . . . ," and on the thirteenth to Berze: "Write to me before the year is out . . ."

On November 21, Father Xavier offered a requiem Mass for a local contrabandist—almost for himself. Two minutes later he was shaken with fever, and leaning heavily on the Chinese, Antonio, he crossed the beach to a small craft which Antonio quickly rowed out to the *Santa Cruz*. But the seas were heavy, and after a night of clinging to his bunk to avoid being tossed about the cabin, he could no longer see. At dawn, exhausted, he asked to be taken ashore, carrying warm clothes under his arm and in his hand a fistful of almonds which he could not even swallow.

A Portuguese merchant, Diego Vaz, had been preparing to leave, but he delayed his departure so that Francis might be bled in his hut. Francis murmured affectionate words of thanks, surrendered to all necessary treatment, and lost consciousness. The fever soon became a delirium in which he talked of trips and friends alike, then, overcome by sudden joy, lapsed into prayer, his head raised, his eyes wide open. Antonio kept watch beside him, but Christopher, his other servant, who was doubtless already planning some thievery, treated him brutally and without respect. With a melancholy gesture, Francis finally sent the man away.

His mind wandered into a curious mixture of Latin, French, Basque, and bits of Tamil or Japanese which had remained in his consciousness. On November 28 he went into a coma, recognizing no one as icy winds blew through apertures in the little hut. The covers Antonio had put over him were blown by gusts—the only bit of motion within the small enclosure. Beside his master, Antonio kept watch.

On December 1, Francis regained consciousness only to resume his prayer. His smile for the faithful Chinese seemed intended for all of China, now beyond his vision. The prayer continued—a vague, indefinite chant—until Saturday, December 3. On that morning, Antonio placed a small candle in his hands.

In the time required to light it, Francis was gone.[61]

Antonio closed his eyes. Then he ran down the beach and, jumping into his boat, rowed out to inform the captain of the *Santa Cruz*. Several officers came ashore to venerate the body, now robed in silk; and the following morning, in lime and a wooden coffin, the apostle was buried on the far side of the island, facing the sea.

When, with the coming of spring, the captain of the *Santa Cruz* weighed anchor, Antonio begged that the body of Francis Xavier be exhumed and carried back to Malacca.

On March 22, when the ship joined the forest of masts in the Malacca harbor, an immense crowd gathered in veneration. The body of the saint was carried up the hill in procession, past a drunken Alvaro da Gama, who was rolling dice with a group of sailors and turned his back on the passing crowd. Within the church, the body was withdrawn from its casket. Shrouded only in his sacerdotal vestments, Francis was laid into the ocher dust of a grave hollowed from the rock itself, close behind the high altar. Today, within the ruined church, this small cave may still be seen. Nearby, torch-red tropical blossoms cluster in the wind, eternally aflame like some lofty tribute to an unknown soldier . . .

Five months later, on August 15, 1553, Diego Pereira, with a Portuguese colleague holding the lantern, came by night to locate and unearth the body of his dear brother and close friend, whom he carried back to his house as a living person.[62] On December 11, in a silken casket, Francis left to go by ship to Cochin and from there as far as Goa.

A strange last chapter for the long adventure: he who had so disliked Goa might well have preferred the red stones of the flowered hill, or the hopeful vistas of Sancian. Humankind so often sees itself as on a pitiless island of destiny, to be carried over tossing seas—by skiff, by junk, by dinghy— towards the shores of an empire which is perhaps security or truth, but surely hope.

To see is but the gift of womankind. God gives the Light. Francis Xavier, dying, had known this hope.

Notes

1. The translation of this passage is that of Brodrick, J., *Saint Francis Xavier*, Doubleday, 1957, p. 18.

2. Where in Germany the appeal of the reform was primarily moral or mystical, reformation and humanism in France were closely allied. Calvin and his disciple, Theodore de Bèze, for example, were counted among the outstanding Hellenists of their time.

3. Ninety-six Jesuits were deported to Dachau. Forty-eight are prisoners in China.

4. Letter from Francis Xavier to Father Barzés, 1549.

5. Favre, *Memorial*.

6. As early as the seventeenth century the crypt of the Martyrium became an inspirational spot where religious leaders, recalling the young Iniguistas, came to meditate on work ahead: Saint Francis de Sales, preparing to found the Order of the Visitation; and Cardinal de Bérulle, that of the Oratorians. The future Lazarists, the first Sulpicians came to pronounce their vows. Abandoned during the French Revolution to a point where Jesuit novices in 1824 were unable to find it, the sanctuary has been completely restored and is visited today by pilgrims from all over the world. Many apostolic projects are drawn up today in the Martyrium.

7. Boehmer, H., *Les Jésuites*, Paris Colin, 1910. Translated as quoted.

8. Monod, Gabriel. A Protestant historian of the nineteenth century, professor at the École Normale Supérieure and Member of the Institut.

9. Brodrick, p. 32.

10. Cf. Brodrick, pp. 31–32.

11. The term at that time was still French.

12. One of the most moving writers of our time, Maxence Van der Meersch, a Catholic tormented by the perils of the human conscience, has written the following, which summarizes what Francis must have thought at the bedside of the unfortunate incurabili:

    "The keyword of our life seems to be love, or gift of self. To accept loss of self, and to gain in the losing—this alone could lead to belief. There are but two loves: love of self, love of other living creatures. Behind love of self lies suffering and evil; behind love of others, God and the Good. Each time that man loves beyond himself, he makes, consciously or otherwise, an act of faith in God. There are but two loves—love of self and love of God."

13. Paul Claudel has observed that, had he himself been a priest, he could not have taken more than an hour of sleep per night.

14. The term was attributed to Charlemagne.

15. There is, nevertheless, something of a risk in any attempted parallel between the first Mass in a dilapidated monastery and a second in the rich décor of Bologna. According to Father Fernet, S.J., the monastery of Vicenza was doubtless abandoned, but the very fact that Saint Francis had been granted the use of it by the Hieronymites shows that they had given official permission for Holy Mass to be offered—either in the old chapel or elsewhere. It is not definitely established that Francis' first Mass was offered on the site of the retreat itself. Father Brou asserts that date and church are both unknown. The ceremony may well have taken place in the city.

16. His form of malaria, while chronic, was fairly mild. The illness was at that time endemic in the southern countries, appearing even in the forest bogs of Normandy. It continues to exist in the coastal areas of almost all hot countries and even in Russia,

Rumania, Greece, Spain, and Italy. It has given rise to many folk tales and has doubtless heightened the French predilection for "visions."

17. Constantinople 717; Poitiers 732; Granada 1492.

18. Cf. Brodrick, p. 43.

19. Ibid., p. 47.

19a. Ibid., p. 44.

20. Paul would be designated, for convenience, by the name of his native town, Camérino.

21. André de Bellessort writes, "Here took place in Ignatius' heart one of those silent dramas by which man succeeds in dying to the affections of the world. The spiritual son, more ready than his father to accept a long trip, resembled any son of any father."

22. Letter of Ignatius Loyola.

23. At the constitutive assembly Favre voted for Loyola, or in case of hindrance or refusal, for Francis Xavier. These votes were prompted by affection. It is doubtful that either Favre or Francis might successfully have replaced Ignatius, for they lacked the administrative genius of the first general. Laynez would logically have been the next best choice.

24. Such signs indicate that Francis was, at this stage of his life, already being honored as a personality and as a person.

25. Despite this sorrow, or perhaps because of it, Faustina was arrogant by nature. Her intent to present Ignatius with a house as a "center" for the Order came to nothing because of the conditions she imposed. The incident, nevertheless, reflects the Jesuit "vogue" only six years subsequent to the secret oath in the Martyrium.

26. These two children died at the ages of seventeen and eighteen.

27. "The court has undergone such reform," Francis wrote to Ignatius, "that it is more like a monastery."

28. The opposition had finally yielded on condition that the Society number no more than sixty members. The promise was willingly given, but the future amply justified its being set aside. At the death of Ignatius, in 1556, the Society numbered one thousand members.

29. Saint Francis' breviary was destroyed on September 16, 1943, in the bombardment of Nantes, which destroyed the house of the Jesuit Fathers.

30. Officers and soldiers, according to a system instituted by Albuquerque for the Orient, were to find women doled out as were food supplies.

31. The *Santiago* sank shortly after.

32. The cross had been erected in 1498 by Vasco da Gama. Hopefully, Alvaro was being authorized by Sousa to gaze on it from a distance.

33. In *La Religion hindoue*, Perrin, Paris, 1954.

34. Brodrick, op. cit., p. 72.

35. Pyrard, François (1570–1621).

36. Cf. Bellessort, André, *Saint François Xavier*, Perrin, Paris, 1918.

37. The college drew its support from the pillaging of Hindu temples. Governors of Portuguese India had orders to destroy insofar as possible these centers of an "idolatrous cult."

38. Francis had obtained from Sousa a modest income of 4,000 small pieces of gold per year for the community of the Paravas.

39. Francis wrote in a letter: "The winds gave me no occasion to return to Cape Comorin; I was obliged to go to San-Thomé." He gives the impression of seeking an excuse for the great joy which he afforded himself.

40. "Our ship raced before a violent wind and constantly scraped the bottom of the sea. If we had struck a rock, the ship would have splintered; with one single shoal we would have gone aground. Many were the tears on board." Thus wrote Francis, adding philosophically further on, "Without the shadow of a doubt, all creation obeys its Creator."

41. "Strange—my love for the Earth. But for the very reason that I feel it so intensely, this depth of the pagan soul, I feel the stronger to speak as an equal with those who worship the Universe—more confident also of the connections and half-reconciliations possible between two passions which I find truly somewhat reconciled within me." Pierre Teilhard de Chardin, *Lettre à Marguerite Teilhard.*

42. "Save for the times of intensive bombardment, when life becomes more animal, concentrated and absorbed in whistling explosions, I have kept a taste for meditation," wrote Pierre Teilhard de Chardin in the worst of Verdun, 1916.

43. André Bellessort. According to Father Brodrick, the princess and the officer had long been secretly in love, and the priest himself had advised the departure.

44. Portugal and Spain were disputing one another's claim to possession of the Philippines.

45. "It is entirely a matter of evidence, and any small boy, busy among the rocks by the seashore, will readily testify that crabs big and small seize bits of stick or other objects thrown to them and scurry off with the prize." Brodrick, p. 159.

46. The name has been variously spelled. Father de Charlevoix writes: Angeroo; Father Brou: Yajro; André Bellessort: Yajirô. Xavier himself—unreliable, since he misspelled all names—wrote: Angero.

47. This incident is placed by some at the moment of Anjiro's first arrival in Malacca in 1546, to free Francis from any responsibility in the affair. This is, moreover, plausible. Writing Ignatius an account of his first contact with the Japanese, Francis is silent about this incident.

48. Cochin was the residence of one of Francis' most intimate friends, the merchant Diego Pereira, whom he called "my true friend."

49. The tribunals of the Inquisition, despite their sinister reputation, were among the most lenient of all tribunals. They nevertheless

represented a firm reaction against the somnolence and lax ways of the clergy, and as such were disturbing to many.

50. Bellessort goes so far as to say that Francis' thirst for open space was simply indicative of an unbalanced mental state. But Bellessort in writing of Francis Xavier, apostle to the Indies, had in reality no sympathy for either Francis or the Indies. His book is flowered with thistles.

51. Today Kyoto.

52. His grandson, a Jesuit, was burned at Nagasaki in 1619 and beatified by Pius IX in 1867.

53. The shores of the Island of Honshu are actually a line of cliffs dominating a seabed 9,435 meters in depth. From these depths to the top of Fujiyama the difference in level is more than 13,000 meters.

54. The bonzes waited long before raising the interdiction on killing —fleas.

55. Miyako and Kyoto have the same meaning: capital. At the time Yedo, the future Tokyo, was only a fishing village.

56. In *Japon*, Arthaud, Paris, 1959.

57. Twenty-seven years later the Daimyo of Bungo would be baptized and bring seventy thousand of his subjects to the new religion.

58. The new Daimyo of Yamaguchi would unfortunately feel obliged to fall on his own sword during the revolution of 1557, after having lent loyal support to Cosmas de Torres for six years.

59. Shortly thereafter Alvaro da Gama was returned to Portugal and given life imprisonment—for having dipped into the royal treasury.

60. Francis wrote: San-Choan.

61. Francis Xavier was aged forty-six years and eight months. His death preceded that of Loyola by four years.

62. The lime in which the body had been buried would keep it incorrupt for over a century.

Francis Xavier was canonized March 12, 1622, by a bull issued by a dying Gregory XV. The document was ratified by his successor, Urban VIII, on August 6, 1623.